T5-BQB-417

The Agricultural Mission
of Churches and
Land-Grant Universities

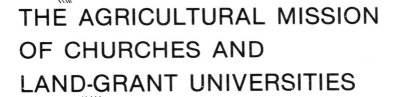

THE AGRICULTURAL MISSION
OF CHURCHES AND
LAND-GRANT UNIVERSITIES

A REPORT
OF AN INFORMAL CONSULTATION

Robert Manning Strozier Library

MAR 3 1980

Tallahassee, Florida

JOHN T. CONNER, CONVENER
DIETER T. HESSEL, EDITOR

THE IOWA STATE UNIVERSITY PRESS, AMES

Soc
HD
9000.6
I49
1978

Robert Manning Strozier Library

MAR 3 1980

Tallahassee, Florida

© 1980 The Iowa State University Press. All rights reserved

Composed and printed by The Iowa State University Press, Ames, Iowa 50010

No part of this publication may be reproduced, stored in a retrieval system, or transmitted, in any form or by any means, electronic, mechanical, photocopying, recording, or otherwise, without the prior written permission of the publisher.

First edition, 1980

Library of Congress Cataloging in Publication Data

Informal Consultation on the Response of Land-Grant Universities to World Hunger,
   Iowa State University, 1978
   The agricultural mission of churches and land-grant universities.

   Includes bibliographical references and index.
      1. Food supply—Congresses. 2. Agriculture—Economic aspects—Congresses.
   3. State universities and colleges—United States—Curricula—Congresses. 4. Church
   and social problems—United States—Congresses. I. Conner, John T., 1927–
   II. Hessel, Dieter T. III. Title.
   HD9000.6.I49   1978   338.1′9   79-17299
   ISBN 0-8138-0920-7

CONTENTS

PREFACE

THE 30 PERCENT of the world's people who live in the developed countries do not have more than their fair share of arable land but they control and consume a disproportionate share of the resources needed for agricultural development. They use 80 percent of all the world's agricultural research funds, 70 percent of the world's chemical fertilizer, and 85 percent of the world's pesticides. They consume 95 percent of the world's petroleum, a significant proportion of which is directed to agricultural uses, and they have about 75 percent of the world's agricultural machinery.

The 70 percent of the world's people who live in the developing countries grow less than 40 percent of the world's food. Moreover, fewer agricultural research dollars are spent in developing countries than are spent in the United States and Canada alone.

Because food production has increased faster than population, we know that those who have the money to buy will have enough to eat. But the gap between effective demand (the market calculus) and human need (the moral calculus) is growing. This gap shows up not only in food consumption, but also in the control of food production. Long-range solutions to the world food crisis must redress this imbalance.

The concerns which led to the chapters in this volume were discussed at an Informal Consultation on the Response of Land-Grant Universities to World Hunger held at the Scheman Continuing Education Center, Iowa State University, Ames, Iowa, March 9-10, 1978. Cosponsors were the Program Agency of the United Presbyterian Church in the USA and the Iowa State University Program in Technology and Social Change in Foreign Cultures. The Task Force on Hunger of the Presbyterian Church in the United States also sent several participants. Costs of the consultation were met by the United Presbyterian Hunger Program, with the intention of facilitating fresh thinking about the role of educators and researchers in the academic disciplines that encompass agriculture and food policy.

PURPOSE AND METHOD

The Ames consultation was convened by John T. Conner, moderator of the 189th General Assembly (1977) of the United Presbyterian Church in the USA (UPCUSA), and campus minister at Oregon State University. He invited pairs of Presbyterian participants—a teacher or administrator, and a campus minister—from ten land-grant schools, plus consultants and staff, to rethink their institution's repsonsibilities in research, curriculum, training, and extension. An intended outcome of the meeting was to produce a report that would foster dialogue and initiative in follow-up gatherings at land-grant universities (LGUs).

The consultation was designed to be a gathering of peers who work in the LGU setting and who want to respond more effectively in their professions to the reality of chronic hunger and malnutrition. The participants were asked to:

1. Review in broad strokes the current response to world hunger by LGUs, with special reference to curriculum emphases, research focus, and training of students from the Third World.

2. Consider the post-Green Revolution responsibility of agricultural schools in relation to poor countries, with particular reference to appropriate research and on-site services.

3. Draw comparisons with parallel concerns in the United States for small farm survival, appropriate technology, and land use policy.

4. Pinpoint innovative designs for curriculum reform in higher education that would make positive, systemic contributions to reduce hunger.

5. Draw implications for campus ministry (CM) at LGUs (and other institutions of higher education that are similarly involved with these matters).

These concerns were explored by discussing brief papers prepared in advance and circulated to the participants. Rather than read the papers at the consultation, each author gave an oral summary of his basic argument and concluded with supplementary comments that initiated an informal discussion among the participants. An edited transcript of that dialogue appears at the end of each chapter. Several of the papers were revised for publication in light of the dialogue.

On the second day of the consultation, the participants formed subgroups to formulate recommendations for the response of the church and the LGU to world hunger. Since the consultation was not a policy-setting body, the recommendations that appear in chapter 10 were referred to the sponsoring denominational agencies. Many of the recommendations are also pertinent for follow-up meetings at LGU's.

OVERVIEW

The style of the consultation was informal; I have tried to preserve that quality in the text, at the risk of omitting the carefully carpentered, qualified language which typifies academic publications.

    The papers and dialogue of this consultation reflect a lively awareness of the appropriate agricultural agenda for the last two decades of the twentieth century. They illumine a particular mission that calls forth the best intentions and resources of two worldwide institutional networks: the church and the university. Both institutional networks are part of the hunger (or food policy) "establishment," in that both have a history of extensive effort to free people from hunger. Both also have a degree of vested interest in particular approaches to the crisis. A refreshing aspect of several chapters in this book is their critique of the strengths and weaknesses of the relevant programs of both university and church. Christians who are active in both settings have a special combination of resources, not the least of which is a global fellowship, enabling them to respond with revived purpose to an urgent problem which requires their best professional expertise.

    Revitalization of *purpose* is the starting point for persons with institutional power. Leaders of church and university tend to become realistic, even to the point of cynicism, about the way things are; rather than to be led by a vision of what ought to be. The moderator's introduction (chap. 1) and the first and last papers of the consultation (chaps. 2 and 9) focus attention on a biblically informed demand for justice toward the poor and oppressed. Both church and university have a role to play in clarifying the values and ideology served by their policies and projects, and in helping to redistribute power and resources for agricultural development among those who have the greatest need. Plants and animals, though indifferent to and impacted by social systems, will thrive accordingly.

    The *problem* explored in the consultation is complex. It is a systemic problem of economic concentration, coupled with disproportionate research and training capability, and sometimes inappropriate technology. In the words of consultant Don Hadwiger:

[The agricultural revolution] is a product of many subsystems as complex and integrated as those that support a spaceship. Agricultural scientists have taken charge of evolution, and to a large extent also of the environment in which growth occurs. Their systems import tons of food for plants and animals, attack insects, diseases, weeds, and other hostile organisms, deliver the output from the farm, and automate the whole endeavor to the point where cropland the size of a county might be handled by fifty or so master farmers.

    Even more involved in this process are the large agribusiness firms that furnish the inputs and process the outputs. Agribusiness firms have relied on the colleges to train the people and provide the technology for their development.

But the industrial agricultural revolution has exacted heavy environmental and human costs. Extensive soil loss, profligate use of water, and heavy chemical pollution portend ominous effects where agriculture has developed and where it is only beginning to develop. Can we identify patterns of agriculture that are environmentally and economically more appropriate to both developing and developed countries? Several of the middle chapters of this book (especially chaps. 3, 4, and 5) point to the possibility of a healthier agriculture that would be as good for us as it is for them. They speak to the nature of agricultural research, as well as its politics, and to the need for poor countries and small farmers to share in the benefits.

As in many other areas of social responsibility, these consultants discern that what we thought was "their" problem—poor countries, small farmers, low-income consumers, peasants—turns out to be "our" problem as rich institutions with misplaced priorities, ecological myopia, disdain for grubby labor, and disregard for the natural, the fragile, the small. Not only is their problem our problem, but their need, in a dramatic way, becomes our need. For our own agriculture is caught up in a cost/price squeeze, spiralling capital debts, and a certain desperation to produce ever more "efficiently" in order to keep up. Our authors use such analogies as "hanging in the top of the willows" or "walking an economic treadmill." Meanwhile, desperate governments and wealthy landlords in developing countries still permit, if not welcome, the same mechanized, energy-land–capital-intensive agriculture, though it drives more people off the land and fails to meet local nutritional needs.

The problem, in short, is that the present pattern has become a no-win game for most people. Changes in the direction of justice would mean benefits for all but the few who now reap short-term profit.

A reconstruction of the agricultural mission of both university and church requires the best *professional* expertise. The redirection of professional expertise, in the eyes of these consultants, entails more research that is free from vested agricultural interests or conventional agricultural methods: Where are the funds for that? Significant reform is equally imperative in the curriculum for all agricultural and other "hard-science" students, particularly international students (see chaps. 6 and 7). The participants in this meeting recognized their power to redesign the training opportunities of a new generation of students to develop moral and political capability as well as technical competence. We must adjust our moral consciousness and apply our technical expertise to a new age of complex interdependencies and systemic outcomes. We can learn how to release more power to exert more influence on the politicians, managers, and scientists who are at the key decision points in dynamic systems. This is a relatively new context for professional behavior that requires interdisciplinary study, evaluative research, planning, organization, and the courage to act in unity with others who perceive the requirements of solidarity.[1]

While the participants in the Informal Consultation on the Response of Land-Grant Universities to World Hunger shared a rather broad consensus, their diagnosis and prescription also reflected some sharp differences over the role of ideology, the stance toward agribusiness corporations, the preferred agricultural alternatives, the role of the public in shaping particular research priorities, and the relevant achievements of the agricultural schools.

But among the participants there was no disagreement about the proper concern and involvement of the Christian community. All seemed ready for the church to do more than its leaders have yet envisioned.

ACKNOWLEDGMENTS

Special thanks are due to all of the participants who took time from busy schedules to respond to Moderator John Conner's invitation; to the authors of the chapters; to Professor George Beran, our host at Iowa State University; to Myrvin DeLapp, who coordinates United Presbyterian involvement in United Ministries in Higher Education (UMHE) and who facilitated the recruitment of participants; to Elizabeth Ryan of the Responsible Agriculture Project, who helped to identify possible consultants; and to Neena Mitchell, who transcribed tapes of the informal discussion and typed this manuscript.

All of us would like this volume to become a resource for study and discussion at many campuses, toward the end that no longer will one out of eight human beings suffer from chronic hunger.

Dieter T. Hessel
Associate for Social Education
United Presbyterian Program Agency
New York, New York

PARTICIPANTS

Colorado State University
 Robert Geller, university pastor
 Lowell Watts, director Extension/Community Services

Cornell University
 William W. Rogers, campus minister
 William E. Gibson, director, Centre for Religion, Ethics, and
  Social Policy

Iowa State University
 Roger Straw, campus minister
 James Clinefelter, associate pastor, Collegiate Presbyterian
  Church
 Don Hadwiger, consultant, and professor of political science
 George Beran, host and professor, College of Veterinary
  Medicine
 Jan Beran, assistant professor, Department of Physical Educa-
  tion

Michigan State University
 S. H. Wittwer, consultant and director/assistant dean, College of
  Agriculture

North Carolina State University
 Steven R. Shoemaker, campus minister
 Gerald A. Carlson, professor of economics (agricultural) and
  business

Oregon State University
 Betsy Baker, campus minister
 Betty Miner, instructor, food and nutrition

Purdue University
 Donald L. Nead, campus minister

University of California at Davis
 Norm Pott, pastor, Davis Community Church
 Paul F. Knowles, professor of agronomy

University of Illinois
    Richard Lundy, pastor/director McKinley Foundation
    Chester Baker, professor of agricultural economics

University of Missouri
    Wendell J. McKinsey, Presbyterian Church, US, Task Force on
        Hunger and assistant dean, College of Agriculture

University of Nebraska
    Lawrence Doerr, campus minister
    A. Dale Flowerday, professor of agronomy

University of Northern Iowa
    Jerry Stockdale, consultant and associate professor, Department
        of Sociology

Other Participants
    Paul Bodine, pastor, St. Paul's Presbyterian Church, LaPorte,
        Iowa
    Kathy and John Conner, Corvallis, Oregon
    Myrvin DeLapp, United Presbyterian Church, USA, Program
        Agency staff
    James Gittings, *AD* magazine
    Tom Haller, United Presbyterian Church, USA, Hunger Pro-
        gram Advisory Committee
    Dieter Hessel, United Presbyterian Church, USA, Program
        Agency staff
    Richard Killmer, staff of the Working Group on Domestic
        Hunger and Poverty, National Council of Churches, New
        York
    Elizabeth Ryan, consultant and director of Responsible
        Agriculture Program, the Action Center, Washington, D.C.

The Agricultural Mission of Churches and Land-Grant Universities

1 INTRODUCTION

JOHN T. CONNER

SOMEONE INTRODUCING ME during my moderatorial travels used the public relations blurb from headquarters and noted that I was moderator of the former Willamette Presbytery (now out of existence), moderator of the former Synod of New Mexico (now out of existence), moderator of the former Synod of Oregon (now out of existence), and present moderator of the General Assembly. I have received some mail which indicated that unless I did something about the particular issues before our church, the General Assembly would surely go out of existence too, and I would be given the entire blame. At least I would go down in history for something.

The focus of my remarks will center around that gospel passage (Matt. 25:35) known as the Great Judgment. ". . . I was hungry and you fed me, thirsty and you gave me drink, a stranger and you welcomed me, imprisoned and you visited me, naked and you clothed me, sick and you ministered unto me"—the various areas of concern for social welfare that our allegiance to Christ calls us to be responsive to. I need not read that familiar passage for us to have it in mind as we gather here. We collect under a small umbrella labeled Hunger; we gather under a larger umbrella labeled Justice; and finally, under the largest umbrella of Christian Responsibility and the mandate Christ laid upon us, particularly in the passage from Matthew.

I would like to quote from two documents. The first document is entitled "Malthus and America," a subcommittee report of the House Agriculture Committee, October 1974. This document is quite familiar on land-grant campuses, certainly on ours, where several thousand were ordered and distributed. In part it reads:

Building quietly and ominously these days is a voice that will rock the world in our lifetime, and that voice articulates the world food and people equation . . . and it is to our blessed land of abundance from across the threshold of scarcity that this voice cries.

John T. Conner was moderator of the 189th General Assembly (1977) of the United Presbyterian Church, USA, and is Campus Minister at Oregon State University, Corvallis, Oregon

3

Will Americans discover too late that Thomas Malthus is a 200-year-old alarmist whose time has finally arrived?

. . . Unless present trends in population growth and food production are significantly altered, a food crisis that will have the potential to affect everyone from every walk of life will hit with more impact than the energy crisis of 1973–74. Unfortunately most of the citizens of this and every country of the world are yet unaware of the phenomenal problem that looms on the horizon. . . .

The world is now also in a uniquely serious situation regarding the supply of land, water, energy, and fertilizer. For the first time in modern history there are shortages of each of these critical agricultural resources. . . . Americans, who heretofore have been rather complacent about this subject, inasmuch as abundant food supplies have been available at low prices in years past and since the growth rate of our population has slowed considerably, cannot afford to sit idly by thinking that this problem does not affect us. . . .

The United States of America, comprising approximately 5 to 6 percent of the world's population, consumes more than 40 percent of the world's resources. The demand for food, like the demand for oil, metals, minerals, and other resources, is obviously going to skyrocket, and that rocket is going to be fueled by fires of inflation and joblessness. . . .

Will America allow a food shortage to surprise us such as we allowed the energy crisis to do this year, and only then react *after* we find people standing in line from 7 A.M. to 9 A.M. on Tuesday and Thursday mornings waiting to get into their local grocery store to buy a limited quantity of food? . . .

The answers aren't easy, but the price of inaction will be cruel.

Think about it, Congress.

Think about it, America.[1]

Quite an unusual and passionate speech coming from the United States Department of Agriculture (USDA). I would like to put that into the context of the remarks of Prime Minister Pierre Trudeau, as he welcomed the official government delegations to the United Nations Conference on Human Settlements (Habitat) held in May 1976. We took a class from Oregon State there; about fifty students and faculty went together for this experience. Trudeau opened his remarks as follows:

There is a new world in the making and a spreading awareness of that fact. No longer can there be a measure of fortune without an equal measure of responsibility. No nation can afford to isolate itself in self-contemplation, clasping to its breast its possessions in denial of others. Human decency requires us to be more open to one another, and modern techniques demand it. No longer is it possible, either morally or technically, not to be accountable. We have entered, willingly or otherwise, the era of a community of interest vital to the survival of the species that has brought us together here.

Trudeau emphasized the interdependence of the world in which we live in his address to the state department delegations of 146 nations of the world. He linked together two words that seem to be somewhat contradictory—conspiracy and love.

It is clear that in order to survive, we will be forced to socialize ourselves more and more. What is actually meant by socializing? From a human point of view it means loving one another. We will thus have not only to tolerate one another, but to love one another in a way that will require of us an unprecedented desire to change ourselves. Such a change will be more drastic than a major mutation of our species. The only type of love that will be effective in a tightly packed world we already live in, will be a passionate love.

That such a statement sounds slightly ridiculous is a measure of the extent of the change we must make if humanity is to survive and thrive.

"Love one another or you will perish," says Teilhard de Chardin, adding that we have reached a critical point in human evolution in which the only path open to us is to move toward a common passion, a conspiracy of love.

What is needed is an intergrated social policy position to be taken by the United States: an integrated, not a piecemeal, social policy approach. Bill Gibson will be stressing this social policy approach in the thesis of his opening paragraph (chap. 2):

. . . that the church and the university, especially the LGU, share a commitment to justice in their dedication to equity, fairness, and the common good; that in both institutions this commitment is maintained precariously and is always threatened by erosion if not abandonment; that the extremity of the world hunger situation constitutes a reassertion of the claim of justice upon both; and that each institution needs to be in partnership with the other, entailing mutual support and mutual criticism, in order to discharge its own responsibility for justice in response to hunger.

In this consultation, we have several things in common. We have in common a relationship to a land-grant institution—although we come from a variety of disciplines. We have sociologists, agriculturalists in various specializations, ag-economists, nutritionists, and theologians represented around this table.

We gather here, however, with another common denominator, as Presbyterians. And it is not with any antiecumenicity that we have been quite specific in inviting Presbyterians to gather around this table, although a couple of you who may not be of that particular persuasion have also been invited. Our principle focus is on the

Presbyterians within these various disciplines, working in land-grant institutions, who need to pay more attention to who they are, their relationships and opportunities, and their mutual need for support. This emphasis is necessary in order that we may experience some sort of symbiosis wherein the responsibilities of our disciplines and our faith commitment may bear rich fruit. It was an awareness of the lack of that relationship and the need to build a bridge that prompted me to suggest to the Hunger Program Advisory Committee and the Program Agency of our church that we call such a consultation as this. Not only is there a mutual concern and offer of mutual support, but there is also the need for a mutual critique. Let us be free, based on our trust and understanding of who we are, to criticize and to try to help each other develop a common response to a common crisis.

For those who are not familiar with the Presbyterian Hunger Program, established officially by the 187th General Assembly (1975) and still in its embryonic stages, it has already achieved significance. That General Assembly established a hunger fund, and the divisions of the money from that fund give some indication of the thrust of Presbyterian concern. Emergency ministry is not our fundamental concern, though we respond to those who are starving and who are in need of food immediately. But for every dollar given to the hunger fund, only thirty cents was given for direct food relief. The balance of the fund supports programs of long-term development, public policy involvement, information, education, and lifestyle modification. The five goals are:

1. To provide maximum amounts of food relief to hungry people, both in this nation and throughout the world.

2. To increase support for projects in the areas of agricultural assistance, health, population stabilization, and other projects for development both in this country and throughout the world.

3. To educate ourselves and others on the hunger crisis and its root causes, including population growth and the distribution of the world's resources, and to develop methods and processes for furthering the commitment of United Presbyterians to deal with the issues of hunger, population and world resources.

4. To adopt lifestyles which consume less of the world's resources and to re-examine the corporate lifestyles of which they are a part.

5. To support changes in United States public policy which will produce more food for hungry people and that will have an impact on

the root causes of hunger, including population growth and the distribution of the world's resources.

In 1977, to reemphasize and to even more strongly emphasize the necessity to deal with systemic causes of hunger, the General Assembly even modified the formula, reducing the direct food relief by five cents on the dollar and increasing by five cents the segment focusing on public policy and education, interpretation, and participation in lifestyle modification. The formula now reads that for every dollar utilized in the hunger fund after administrative expenses are taken out (in 1977, the administrative expenses for that fund were just a little over 9 percent), the remaining $2 million annually is to be divided—twenty-five cents for direct food relief, fifty-five cents for long-term development, and twenty cents for public policy education, interpretation, and lifestyle modification.

People in Congress know how important it is for church people to be involved in the public policy dimensions of human rights, human justice, and the issue of hunger. Senator Dick Clark of Iowa, on his return from the 1974 Rome food conference, commented that neither the Congress nor the Administration were interested in significant follow-up legislation until the largest outpouring of letters hit Congress since the Cambodian bombing. These letters came, significantly, from the church people across our country. Clark noted and bemoaned the fact that Congress had added that year, without too much debate, an eleventh Trident submarine to its fleet, costing at that time $1.6 billion. He stressed that this was almost the identical amount utilized for the food development aid worldwide through Public Law 480, and he prefaced his remarks, saying:

I am just as interested in national security as anyone, but I would suggest that when you can destroy the world fourteen times over already, adding another Trident isn't going to do that much to deter aggression. But perhaps doubling the world food aid budget would be a significant deterrent to aggression.

Could it be that we are much more threatened by hungry bellies in the world than we are by H bombs? The noted economist, Barbara Ward, has suggested that if we would take that $3 billion saved by reducing arms budgets 1 percent worldwide and apply it to providing potable water worldwide, that a miracle could be performed in a decade. I was reminded of that when we were in Pakistan recently and saw the women lining up at the wells loading not one, but two large jars on top of their heads and then walking better than a mile, sometimes several miles, to get the water home.

When I visited with Senator Mark Hatfield recently, he reaffirmed his interest in something that we've been doing in the most embryonic stages at Oregon State—offering a few courses in peace science and in peace education. Two of our graduates from Oregon State came to the platform at the General Assembly in Philadelphia, when I was elected moderator, shook my hand, and reminded me that they had taken several courses we offered at Oregon State in peace science. Now they are enrolled in the Ph.D. program in peace studies at the University of Pennsylvania. I shared this incident at Princeton University recently, and there happened to be a pastor visiting the chapel that day. I have just received a letter from him about his search for advanced study in this area, and as a result of those remarks, he went to the University of Pennsylvania to talk to the head of the department. He is now enrolled in their doctoral program in peace science.

I mention peace science particularly because it speaks to the mandate of the land-grant institutions established under the Morrill Act of 1862. There are three primary ingredients in the act, increased in scope by subsequent legislation: agricultural assistance and leadership in our local areas and the development of outreach and extension programs in the states provided by the Smith-Lever Act (1914); funding for training in the industrial and mechanical arts; and the implementation of the requirement that every land-grant institution provide "instruction in the military sciences." I shared with Senator Hatfield my dream that some day the Morrill Act might be amended to require LGUs to provide instruction in the peace sciences. There may be some other major amendments that we, who are talking and thinking about the major dimensions of land-grand institutions, might scrutinize. At least we ought to examine whether or not some adjustment in the act for the security and enhancement of society is necessary today.

T. S. Eliot in his play, *Murder in the Cathedral,* observes: "The last temptation is the greatest treason—to do the right deed for the wrong reason." I would suggest that there is an appropriate amount of loyalty to our institutions, both church and university, and yet if the reason for loyalty is the preservation of the institution itself, then of course it is the wrong reason and is the greatest treason. We might well examine the premises upon which our churches and universities exist, and how our institutions reflect a fundamental concern for the presence of injustice in society, especially in regard to our relations with the poor nations of the world.

I am interested in emphasizing the possibilities for social change that frequently exist within our institutions, and not the obstacles in our way. When I went to Oregon State it was quite a revelation to me, because I had pictured in my mind's eye, a strong unity there. I had been in a ministry in New Mexico where I was troubled by the major chasms between the various religious institutions. In Oregon, I found that these chasms existed within the university as well. I would hope that our consultation might build bridges of common support and common effort.

I expressed those aims in my letter of invitation:

I want this meeting to be a gathering of peers who work in the land-grant college setting and who want to respond more effectively in their professions to the reality of chronic hunger and nutrition. I am inviting pairs of participants—a teacher or administrator, and a campus minister—from ten land grant schools, plus consultants and staff, to begin a process of rethinking our institutions' responsibilities. One outcome of our meeting will be a report that may foster dialogue and initiative in curriculum, training, research, extension, as well as follow-up meetings at land grant schools.

Can we touch—permeate is probably too ambitious—but at least touch a major segment of the whole land-grant network through clergy and laity who have a commitment to doing something about the injustice of hungry people in the world? Can we replicate this event at Cornell or at other institutions? It is possible that the University of California at Davis may have some way of reaching down to the universities in Arizona. I met with the faculty of Arizona State University recently. They asked if they could attend the conference in Ames. Since we were limiting our consultation to LGUs, I said no, but I explained that someone would be glad to come and discuss the subject after the conference.

This expressed interest must not be an isolated experience. We should plan to achieve a ripple effect, by sharing our deliberations in print, and by stimulating fresh dialogue within our institutions. I simply offer these remarks as an overview. We come together with diverse professional expertise. Yet we come together with the common goal that we may fulfill the admonition to feed the hungry, clothe the naked, and respond to the problems of unjustice and inequity in our world.

2 JUSTICE, THE CHURCH, AND THE LAND-GRANT UNIVERSITY

WILLIAM E. GIBSON

THE THESIS of this chapter is that the church and the university, especially the LGU, share a commitment to justice in their dedication to equity, fairness, and the common good; that in both institutions this commitment is maintained precariously and is always threatened by erosion, if not abandonment; that the extremity of the world hunger situation constitutes a reassertion of the claim of justice upon both; and that each institution needs to be in partnership with the other, entailing mutual support and mutual criticism, in order to discharge its own responsibility for justice in response to hunger.

JUSTICE AS A COMMON COMMITMENT
The church's commitment to justice is an integral part of the life of a people responding in faith to the God who calls them into a relationship of faithfulness. Christians believe that in Jesus Christ, God "gets through" to them with a love that judges and liberates, as they respond in repentance, trust, and obedience. The deity who thus calls them immediately points them to their neighbors. To relate faithfully to God means to relate lovingly to human beings; and that means to care about them, to will what is good for them, all of them. Justice may be defined as love distributed to all one's neighbors. It has to be embodied in the institutions and structures whereby societies are organized for various human purposes; and the ultimate social unit is global, the one family of humankind. The human family, moreover, must understand and affirm its interdependence with the natural world. One's "neighbors" are the whole creation, human and nonhuman. Justice means respect, fairness, and concern toward all. For as Dean Freudenberger and Joseph Hough put it, "God created the world and called humankind to live together for the good of each other and the earth."[1]
In order to suggest a sufficiently broad conception of justice,

William E. Gibson is coordinator of the Eco-Justice Project, Centre for Religion, Ethics, and Social Policy, Ithaca, New York.

Freudenberger and Hough utilize the idea of the "common good." From a Christian perspective they see the sought-for common good as a "world in which all people have access to the basic necessities of life, in which all people have some say about the shape of their future, and where decisions about resource use stand under the judgment of some assessment about the renewable carrying capacity of the earth."[2]

The church is committed to justice in the sense that its members are called to serve the common good. The church, moreover, speaks to society in behalf of the common good. In so doing it does not assume that everyone shares the church's theological foundation for espousing and doing justice, but only that since everyone belongs to this created order (in which God acts to judge and redeem), the claims of justice are inescapable. These claims are the claims of every person, every creature, and the earth itself to be treated with respect, fairness, and concern.

The university is also committed to promoting the common good. This is implicit in the university's own statement of purpose and mission. The most explicit commitment of the university is to the transmission and extension of knowledge; but knowledge, however much it may be valued for its own sake, is instrumental to other purposes. Knowledge is properly subject to the claims of justice.

The establishment of land-grant colleges, as the result of the Morrill Act of 1862, was a landmark in the democratization of higher education. It made a university education both more available and more practical. Its benefits were no longer to be reserved for a privileged few, who might then use them in service to society, but were now to be put increasingly within the reach of common folk. Their educational advancement would serve the accelerating development of the nation's agriculture and industry. As time went by, the mission of the land-grant colleges was enlarged to include pioneering programs of research in agriculture and then extension services whereby the results of that research might have wide-scale application to the nation's farms. The colleges, of course, went on to do research and provide extension services in many fields. The emphasis on agriculture, however, was and is indicative of their commitment to address the most basic need of all—the food and nutrition necessary for life and health. Certainly it was and is their intention to assist the farmers to produce food for all. That indeed was and is a commitment to justice.

EROSION OF COMMITMENT

Although societies are under a claim to make their institutions and structures serve the needs of all, that claim is continually at odds with individual and collective greed. The structures are power structures, devised and manipulated by those who wield the power, so that the common good gets subordinated to narrow interests and private profit—unless the power is balanced or diffused. "We know," said Reinhold Niebuhr, "that business and politics are not governed by unselfishness." Hence the rough justice that we have, even though it reflects the sense of responsibility toward family, nation, and humankind, has "transmuted" that responsibility into "various balances of power in order to prevent the strong from taking advantage of the weak, by making the weak a little stronger but not too strong."[3]

In the modern world the "strong" who control the structures and take advantage of the weak are not located in the church or in the university (generally speaking), but in the giant corporations. Even government power is subordinate and subservient (on the whole) to the power that flows from the highly concentrated wealth of multinational firms exercising oligopolistic control over production-distribution processes. The expressed purpose of these firms is the maximization of profit which is tied to, and perhaps even subordinated, temporarily, to the growth of the firms and the strengthening of their control over supply, land, technology, labor, finance, and marketing. The maximization of profit, though it generates much activity that addresses human needs and wants, is not compatible with the maximization of the common good. More profits are to be gained in catering disproportionately to the wants of some than in giving chief consideration to the basic needs of all.

The erosion of the commitment to justice in church and university does not reside in a conscious decision against the common good. It lies partly in the limitations of their perceptions of what it takes to achieve justice; partly in the difficulty of making shifts in programs and priorities to serve the cause of justice better; and partly in their own dependence upon the very structures of power that perpetuate injustices. The vulnerability of church and university to these limitations reflects an insufficient clarity and sureness regarding the nature and insistence of the claims of justice.

The self-understanding of the church may lead those who speak for it to say that the church's "business" is "salvation," without making clear (or even being clear) that "saved" persons necessarily are called into the struggle for justice. The love commandment is given a severely restricted interpretation in terms of decency, kindness, and evangelism, without ever confronting converts with the consistent and insistent biblical translation of love as compassion toward, ministry to, and identification with, the poor, the weak, the vulnerable, the hungry, the strangers, the prisoners, the oppressed—that is to say, the victims of injustice.

The reasons for this truncated transmission of the Christian message are not hard to find. Love-inclusive-of-justice is costly. It entails not merely relief for the needy, but the transformation of the unjust structures that keep people needy. That means it will be resisted fiercely by the powerful who benefit disproportionately from present arrangements. A commitment to justice gets a person or an institution into controversy and struggle. The way to maximize justice may be unclear, and it is easy to feel powerless before the forces of resistance to change. The changes sought may threaten the position and the security of the church itself and its individual members, especially its leaders and its leading financial supporters. Institutional self-preservation stands as a formidable obstacle to the church's expression of its commitment to justice at the points where the forces that victimize our neighbors and ourselves are most cruel and resistant.

The university's self-understanding may lead those who speak for it to say that the "business" of the university is "knowledge"—passing it on and gaining more—without making clear (or even being clear) that a moral responsibility necessarily goes along with knowing. The responsibility includes but transcends honesty and objectivity in gathering and weighing data. It includes, also, the sharing of the benefits from what is or can be known. It includes sensitivity to conditions in the world at the points where knowledge-as-power is most needed for the rectification of inequities. Through a host of decisions about what shall be communicated and investigated and who finally shall be served by teaching and research, the university's true commitments are revealed.

It is exceedingly risky for the university to stand unequivocally for the employment of knowledge for the extension of justice. Sooner or later it leads professors and students into the difficult, complex, controversial issues that pertain to the redistibution of economic and political power. As in the church, here too the examination of such issues proves threatening to those who have a vested interest in existing structures. Faculty and staff learn to avoid offense toward those whose favor can determine their own security and advancement. Once again, self-preservation, institutional as well as individual, erodes the commitment to justice at the points where it could be most applicable to the struggles of the poor.

Both the church and the university have a depoliticized understanding of the nature of their tasks. The representatives of these institutions know that they are not the chief wielders of power in the modern world. They feel that they did not create the unjust structures and that they are not the chief beneficiaries of the gross inequities. For the most part they feel that they are essentially powerless to change things in any fundamental way. Christians fall back upon "justification by faith" and hold to the thought that in a strictly private transaction with God they have been forgiven for whatever complicity they may have in the miseries of the poor. The academic falls back upon the justification accruing to competence in a professional discipline, neglecting its points of intersection with the realities of the rich-poor gap. Academic and churchman alike may feel that nonparticipation in struggle and controversy has kept them from corruption.

Such understandings serve well the preservation of the status quo, if not the intensification of present sufferings. Dorothee Soelle in developing a "political theology" understands "the sinner [as] the collaborator . . . of a structurally founded, usually anonymous injustice." From this point of view there is no purity through noninvolvement but rather the "sin [of] *collaboration* and *apathy*." [Emphasis added.] She goes on to say that for these to be recognized "theology must have the help of the human sciences, insofar as they provide information about the possibilities of alternative behavior."[4] We cannot profess powerlessness before the forces of injustice. The illusion of powerlessness is the false basis of an easy conscience.

HUNGER AS THE CHALLENGE TO RENEWED COMMITMENT

In 1973–1974 the phenomenon of mass hunger, malnutrition, and actual starvation in the poor, less developed countries of the world became so gigantic and obscene that hunger became the subject of an unprecedented media blitz. The churches committed themselves to address more seriously than ever before the issues of world hunger. LGUs received similarly a new impetus to strengthen and accelerate their programs bearing upon the problems of producing and distributing food for all.

Today, after a few years of improved harvests, the situation appears to have lost its crisis character. We have returned in some ways to the pre-1973 situation, when "only" 462 million people were suffering from an insufficient protein-energy supply according to Food and Agriculture Organization estimates.[5] The figure is almost certainly higher now. Nevertheless, the situation appears superficially to have improved somewhat; starvation is at least more gradual. The most conspicuous sign of a return to some sort of "normalcy" is that United States agricultural policies must once again deal with the problem of surpluses—the excess production that is excessive, not because the half-billion or so protein-energy deficient people could not use it, but because they have no effective purchasing power with which to buy it, and because we could not give it to them (even if we thought we could afford to do so) without undermining our balance of payments and their progress (if any) toward food self-sufficiency.

The irony is that "in the Third World, on the whole, there is more food and less to eat."[6] The methods of the "Green Revolution" (mechanization, irrigation, and large inputs of chemical fertilizers and pesticides), together with the expansion of the activities of agribusiness corporations into developing countries, have worked against the viability of small-scale farming, thus forcing rural people off the land, cutting them out of production and therefore out of consumption.[7] The additional food that is produced is not even intended for the hungry people of the country. The profits for the corporations and the local elite lie in converting from crops for home consumption to vegetables, fruits, beef, and carnations for export to Europe and America.

The problem of hunger persists because poverty persists. National and international economic systems do not permit access by all to the means of obtaining the minimum necessities. They have no mechanisms for distributing among all the people the food supplies that in fact are sufficient for all people. They deprive vast numbers of the land on which they might produce food for themselves and then provide no alternative employment whereby they might purchase what they need.

If we call the hungry by their right names, says Dorothee Soelle, we shall call them *"those we let starve."*[8] In other words, we tolerate, and collaborate with, systems that keep them down. Denis Goulet observes that the developed world (including the privileged class in poor countries) "has legitimized its structures of greed by invoking the necessity, and the merits, of the market system." He insists that "an international order founded on the market system . . . is inherently unable to solve the hunger and scarcity problems at their roots."[9]

The challenge confronting both the church and the LGU is this: Do they find hunger, malnutrition, and starvation so intolerable that they will venture at last to probe the problems to their roots? That would be a renewal of their commitment to justice. It would be risky and costly. It would put all decisions about program in the context of concern for justice.

POSSIBILITIES OF PARTNERSHIP

A policy statement of the Governing Board of the National Council of Churches states well some of the underlying causes of the world food crisis. Most of the acute hunger in the world is the legacy of "economic colonialism"—the economic domination of poor countries by rich countries, a domination which has continued after the disappearance of political colonialism. The statement cites the unregulated operations of multinational corporations, the unfair terms of international trade, the inappropriate development of capital-intensive agricultural systems, the foreign aid programs designed to benefit the donors more than the recipients, and the forms of food relief that foster dependency and discourage self-reliance. Closely related to all of these is the insufficient, often distorted development of agriculture in many Third World countries. Market forces have encouraged the cultivation of a single crop for export rather than the balanced production of food for home consumption. Land reform and credit reform are long overdue. Frequently agriculture has gotten a lower national priority than industrial development, tourism, and military needs.[10]

The church in the context of a renewed commitment to justice needs the partnership of the LGU in addressing the underlying, root causes of world hunger. It needs the expertise of the university to help it tell the story of hunger "like it is." It recognizes the enormous potential of the LGU to contribute to the fundamental solutions of the problems: (1) through university's training of students from the Third World in agriculture and other disciplines; (2) through its research programs in international agriculture and the overseas rural development projects in which it engages; (3) through its general educational offerings, whereby large numbers of students from many fields, as well as many other persons participating in cooperative extension programs, may be informed of the realities of world hunger and its root causes; and (4) through overall institutional policies whereby all teaching, research, and outreach may be infused with the kind of commitment to justice that encourages a penetrating critique of unjust systems, together with a determined search for strategies and policies that would bring about a transformation.

More specifically, the church looks to the university now for a holistic approach to world food issues, within which there would be at least these major focuses:

1. Food self-sufficiency for the poor. The assumption is that we have ample evidence now to be convinced that justice will be served by development policies that seek sufficiency through empowering small farmers to improve production for their own use and/or benefit. In many countries land reform is desperately needed, so that small plots can be made available to many farmers. Even so, we are informed that a billion people presently receive their livelihood from farms of five hectares or less. Sylvan H. Wittwer stresses this potential (chap. 3):

"Technologies addressed to small scale, labor intensive, capital, and resource sparing farming would capture an unexploited food production frontier. . . . The output per hectare of these mini-holdings can significantly exceed that of the large U.S. farms."

This development, however, depends upon resistance to the encroachments of multinational agribusiness. In order to help meet the needs of poor people, the university may have to pursue a policy of noncooperation in any project that furthers the agribusiness practice of taking over large holdings for export crops.

According to Sylvan H. Wittwer, this suggests a major shift in research priorities, inasmuch as almost all agricultural research in this country is "still directed to large scale commercial or modern agriculture." Moreover, it suggests that when economic and political structures operate to keep poor people from reaping the benefits of agricultural research and development aid, those structures and the means and problems of changing them become the proper and compelling objects of social-scientific investigation by the LGU.

2. Appropriate agricultural technology. The United States model of agricultural development is highly energy-intensive, fossil-fuel-dependent, capital-intensive, mechanized, and labor-saving. This model may have served us well (up till now), but it is not what Third World countries need. They need smaller, less expensive, less sophisticated technologies, adapted to local conditions, utilizing the large supply of human labor, and designed therefore to enhance that labor and make it more productive without replacing it. Such technologies are based on renewable sources of energy and a harmonious relationship with the natural environment.

Again, the emphasis upon such technologies entails resistance to agribusiness and a de-emphasis on those technologies associated with the Green Revolution insofar as they are tailored only to the large, capital-intensive farm.

Obviously there are profound implications here for the kind of development assistance provided by this country, and for the kind of training offered to Third World farmers and students.

3. Ecologically sustainable farming methods. This focus is needed in our own country at least as much as elsewhere. It is required for doing justice to soil, air, water, and natural systems and also to the future generations to whom we ought to pass a habitable planet. The most obvious need is to reduce dependence on diminishing supplies of ever more expensive fossil fuels. This means reducing inputs of synthetic fertilizers, pesticides, and herbicides and returning to organic methods of farming. It also means water conservation and the protection of the soils from erosion and deterioration.

To focus on ecologically sustainable farming methods would be a reversal of trend, according to Don F. Hadwiger (chap 4), for up till now "the research establishment has been less than eager to anticipate resource scarcities . . . [and] has usually ignored environmental costs."

4. Strengthening the small farmer in the United States. Here too it is important from the standpoint of justice to stop and reverse the trend toward ever greater concentrations of economic power in agriculture, food processing, and marketing. The number of small, independent farmers has diminished steadily for decades. These people, hit especially hard now by soaring costs, have seldom had a fair deal relative to other sectors of the economy. Revisions in the tax and inheritance laws, together with legislation to set parity at or near 100 percent, would help them to stay in farming. The land-grant university should give highest-priority attention to the needs and problems of small farmers, recognizing that agriculture has entered a new era in this country with a new set of imperatives to be faced if small family farms are to withstand the powerful competition of big commercial agriculture. The college can multiply its efforts to help small farmers cope with rising costs, to strengthen their efforts to protect their fragile resources of soil, water, and air, and to improve the feasibility of organic agriculture, assisting them to get started on the inevitable transition to a greatly reduced dependence on fossil fuels.

In the partnership with the LGU, the church can offer its theological perspectives and ethical insight, a significant network for education and communication, and political support for the shifts in the teaching, research, and outreach priorities that it calls upon the university to make.

Church and university need each other's criticisms, as the university helps the church to relate its ideals and visions to factual data and scientific insights into social process, and the church reminds the university of the moral responsibility to apply knowledge to the common good.

The campus minister serves appropriately as agent and broker of this partnership, bringing people together, facilitating the exchange of ideas and insights, and insisting on the responsibility of all to deal with root causes and hard, controversial, systemic problems. He or she may even have some role in offering the spiritual resources that can protect both institutions from being overwhelmed by the impulse to self-preservation, or paralyzed by the illusion of powerlessness, or mired by default in collaboration with injustice.   ●

INFORMAL DISCUSSION

Gibson: The problem of hunger is the problem of poverty, and the prevalence of poverty reflects upon the systems under which we do our business and whereby the goods which people need are distributed. I keep running into people who talk about the way our economic system works—as though they were describing a natural law that has to be accepted and adjusted to, rather than a problem to be solved. The challenge as I see it now is whether we do believe that the system as it exists is intolerable, and therefore whether the concern for food, food for all, must indeed take precedence over the many considerations that often stand in the way of distributing food resources to everyone who is in need. I do not mean handing it out, but enabling people to have access to the land and to the technology, the necessary resources; to move toward their own capacity to either grow or buy what they need. The concern for justice may take precedence over the various considerations that stand in its way, particularly the interests that represent wealth and power which are always ready to use the church and university for their purposes and to object to the critique that may be made in either institution, to the effect that the systems under which we are living are indeed unjust and do not serve the common good.

Knowles: Just one comment, question. You singled out the corporate farms as being ogres in this situation. I think we should not separate out corporate farms from corporate anything else. I think many businesses have entered the orbit of large multinational corporations. So are we saying that in business that's OK, but when it comes to farms, it's not OK?

Gibson: No, I don't intend to do that. My first reference to corporate structures was not geared to farming in particular but to the power of giant corporations in general, and indicated my own conviction that there is an incompatibility between maximization of profit and maximization of the common good—that the interests served if profit is the overriding consideration, in instance after instance, are injurious to the common good. This does not mean there may not be some place for market mechanisms within the kind of system which might be more serviceable, but I did not try to spell that out.

Shoemaker: If the locus of the greatest amount of economic power is in the hands of certain large corporations of various kinds, and if justice is sometimes defined as the balance of power, where is the balance of power to come from? You suggested that most of the economic power at the present time is in the hands of large coporations, so I'm wondering how can justice be accomplished?

Gibson: Well, that's the statement of the problem. The countervailing power is not sufficient. I think government is a countervailing power, and that government is the only agency we have that has both the responsibility and the capability to do some of the planning and to undertake some of the measures that are necessary. But the problem is that, once again, governments are subordinated to corporate power, and that means that the public as a whole has got to organize and insist that government power be exercised in the common good, instead of in the good of special interests.

Knowles: I don't want to appear as an advocate of large corporations, but I assume you are thinking primarily of the banana republic? I've been to at least one country where the government couldn't introduce hybrid corn and make it profitable in the community, but the corporation wanted this product and it wanted it for sale locally, and the corporation brought in or hired their best local researcher and the best sort of administrative organization. And it wasn't very long until the community was growing hybrid corn and the yields of that area were much higher than in other areas of Pakistan. This corporation with some ingredient of self-interest, but also with some larger concern, was able to do what the government could not do. It seems to me we have to be very careful when we criticize the corporations because some of them can do some things in countries that the governments simply can't do.

Gibson: I'm not trying to suggest that there is never any coincidence of profitability and the common good, but that when profits are the overriding consideration in instance after instance this works against the availability of land, of crucial inputs and markets, and of food to the people who are most in need of it. I'm thinking of countries in Central and South America, where land is taken over for growing carnations, beef, or vegetables, all for export and profit. People are not able to have access to land for their own subsistence, nor are they able to find employment in order to buy food, and while there may be more food produced in the country itself, there is less food for the people who are there.

Stockdale: I think your point is well taken—switching from the term corporation to the term profit is appropriate. The whole developed world is something like a "city"; it goes out and uses its hinterland to supply what it needs. It seems to me that's very much the situation we're involved in when we talk about developed and Third World countries. The politics is important. The politics of local countries influences whether or not countries are willing to be a part of our hinterland. In terms of countervailing force, it's unfortunate that in Third World countries sometimes the only option that seems viable to protesting groups is to go socialist or communist so they won't have to be the hinterlands anymore. We must think more clearly about socio-economic means by which people can take care of themselves. The view that a lot of countries seem to be faced with is: Are we going into the orbit of the communist block and feed our own people, or are we going to stay in the other orbit and feed the developed countries? Maybe that's a false picture.

Gibson: I hope that's a false way of posing it.

Bodine: We need to be concerned about larger corporations buying small farms. I know we've had laws trying to protect small farms from large corporations because of the very fact that larger corporations find it to their economic benefit to plow under food as a tax write off. The vested interests of larger corporations when they buy farms are not the same as the interests of small farmers, so it might be to their advantage to plow under for tax reasons.

Gibson: The motivation is for the profit of the enterprise rather than for getting food to people who need food.

C. Baker: Where is it the corporations are buying so much farmland? In some states they have been reducing their holdings of land, because they have a better use for the money.

Conner: Wasn't the Merrill Lynch proposal one that was shot down because government interceded?

C. Baker: This wasn't a corporation purchase, as such. They were going to invest some pension funds.

Gibson: Of course that's only one aspect of the concentration of the economic power in food production, marketing, and processing. Control can be exercised through "forward contracts" without actual ownership. It would be misleading to talk about land being the only, or even the main aspect of corporate economic power in this country.

C. Baker: United Fruit has sold their land in Central America because it is not a good deal for them.

Wittwer: Large corporations in agriculture have not been noticeably successful in this country. The Soviets have tried it for forty years; it doesn't work very well. Consider one point also with respect to the matter of commodities (cash crops) produced in foreign countries. Much of the investment in terms of agriculture research in developing countries has been and still is directed toward nonfood items.

Doerr: I'm wondering how helpful it really is to say in any descriptive or operationally meaningful sense that the church or university as an institution is committed to justice and some sense of equity. Certainly they ought to be, but I am not sure we really do ourselves a favor and see with clear glasses when we say that as institutions, or with any major thrust of the weight of their operations, either church or university works for justice. I want to push you on that a little bit.

Gibson: I think we are on the same wavelength in talking about the precariousness with which this commitment is held, and the fact that when you get into justice questions you get into controversial questions, and neither the church nor the university institutionally welcomes controversial questions. Many of those whose money the church depends upon, as well as those whose money the university depends upon, are precisely the people who are benefiting from present arrangements. Therefore it is very difficult for either institution to be consistent in telling it like it is; exposing the reality that exists and ' addressing those things as problems to be solved, as instances of conditions that have to be changed, rather than conformed to.

Doerr: I guess I'm raising the question right at that point. Does it really help us to say there's a basic commitment here, and if we kind of get ourselves clear about what's going on, this commitment is going to express itself like a tidal wave? I feel instead that there are some people within both institutions who are always fighting a guerilla, or rear guard, action in order to make that kind of commitment find expression institutionally.

Gibson: I think this is true. On the other hand, there is a claim that justice makes upon both institutions to which these people you are talking about, who are a minority, can always appeal—and an appeal should be made. I don't know why the church has launched a hunger program, unless it is out of a concern for justice. There's no other reason for the church to do this, unless it remains strictly within the area of humanitarian relief. But the program is not just geared to humanitarian relief, which is one-fourth of the whole program.

Flowerday: I interpreted your presentation here as designed to raise questions about industrial complexes, corporations, even agbusiness corporations. Is that true?

Gibson: That was what I was trying to say in response to some of the questions.

Flowerday: I think as we examine the power in those structures we will find that we are all a part of those structures, if we look at where we have invested some of our retirement funds. So when we begin to hack away, we need to know what we're hacking at.

Gibson: But it's not a natural law that pension funds have to invest in corporations that ignore basic principles of corporate responsibility and social justice.

3 APPROPRIATE AGRICULTURAL TECHNOLOGIES AND LAND-GRANT UNIVERSITIES

SYLVAN H. WITTWER

FOOD IS one of our most important renewable resources. The United States contributes about one-third of the over $4 billion world expenditure on agricultural, food, and nutrition research.[1] But poverty and malnutrition continue as global problems. To this end, the role of the LGUs of America in agricultural development needs reassessment.

There have been many studies on needs and priorities for agricultural development in poor countries and, to a lesser extent, for the poor farmers with limited resources in our country. World food conferences have been held and proceedings published.[2,3] Numerous congressional hearings have been sponsored.[4,5,6] Priorities for agricultural food and nutritional research have been established.[7,8,9,10,12] In addition, gaps have been identified.[9,11,12,13] A series of recommendations for improved management—organizational prerequisites, operational strategies, institutional changes—have been assembled.[11,12,14] New legislation (Title XII of the Foreign Assistance Act of 1975; Title XIV of the Food and Agriculture Act of 1977) provides a base for initiation of new agricultural, food, and nutrition research in developing countries and at home with the participation of the LGU system. Other United States agencies now have decision centers and programs on food production for farmers of limited resources, and on international agricultural research to better identify appropriate roles in food research. The Steering Committee Report of the National Academy of Sciences' World Food and Nutrition Study, with its twenty-two research priorities, suggests that there is the need, prompted by rising populations and increased affluence in developing countries, to increase food production from 3 to 4 percent per year until the end of this century.[12] This compares to a past (1950–1975) average performance of only 2.8 percent per year.

Sylvan H. Wittwer is director, Agricultural Experiment Station; assistant dean, College of Agriculture and Natural Resources; and professor of horticulture, Michigan State University, East Lansing, Michigan.

DECLINE IN AGRICULTURAL PRODUCTIVITY

Ironically, this comes at a time when the productivity of the major food crops in the United States has plateaued. Yields of wheat, maize, sorghum, soybeans, and potatoes have not increased since 1970. This is true, also, of maize, potatoes, wheat, rice, and cassava in Latin America and much of Southeast Asia and Africa. World grain yields have declined. It comes also at the very time when we are faced with an overabundance of food, huge surpluses, and farm prices below the cost of production. The recent increase in food production has been achieved as a result of unusually good weather on a global scale and by cropping more land.

This phenomenon needs careful analysis. Farm yields rose rapidly in the United States following World War II. These were accompanied by technologies requiring massive inputs of fossil energy channeled to the farm as fertilizer, pesticides, irrigation, mechanization, and new seeds. Greater production efficiency was the goal. The result was plentiful food at low cost.

While the words of Jonathan Swift in *Gulliver's Travels* still hold, "and he gave it for his opinion that whoever could make two ears of corn, or two blades of grass, to grow upon a spot of ground where only one grew before would deserve better of mankind and do more essential service to his country than the whole race of politicians put together . . ." we must now not only produce two ears of corn and two blades of grass where but one grew before, but we must do it in a way that is sparing in the use of land, water, energy, fertilizers, and pesticides. All of these external inputs, with the possible exception of genetic improvements, are becoming increasingly costly, subject to more constraints, and less available. Some come from nonrenewable resources. Most all existing agricultural technology in the United States has been developed during an era characterized by declining energy costs.[15] The high agricultural output of the United States has been closely tied to the availability of fossil fuel inputs. Direct spin-offs of high energy agriculture include increased specialization (monoculture), reduced redundancy, less resiliency, and a movement away from small- and medium-sized producing units.

Meanwhile, soil erosion continues unabated nationally and globally. After forty years of a United States soil conservation program, no more than 25 percent of our farmlands are cultivated under approved conservation practices. Topsoil continues to be lost at an enormous rate. Soil organic matter is being reduced. There is greater compaction from excess and untimely tillage. Chemical residues in soils may be having an impact. Air pollution is becoming more severe. Additional land areas brought into cultivation may be less productive. With increasingly greater pressures on the productive land resource base, the options for use of water, fertilizer, pesticides, and mechanization become progressively less.

Some would credit the recent plateauing of crop yields to adverse and fluctuating climate and weather. Season-to-season variations, however, are far more significant than any identifiable long-term trends. Regulatory and financial constraints on the use of labor, chemicals, water, and energy are increasingly costly and stifle production. Finally, there has been a twelve-year erosion of the federal investment in agricultural research, not only in manpower, but in new equipment and facilities. Enrollments in the colleges of agriculture in the LGUs have tripled in ten years, with little, if any, increase in faculty. Science years in support of agricultural research have not changed since 1966. Teaching needs had to be met. As a consequence, research was left behind.

STABILITY OF FOOD PRODUCTION

There are problems in stability of food supply, rivaling those for increased productivity. Instability results from both biotic and environmental stresses; chemical, environmental, and genetic vulnerability of crop varieties and breeds of livestock; and lack of technology for drying and storage of indigenous production.

INTERNATIONAL AGRICULTURAL RESEARCH CENTERS

We now face the reality of an extraordinary rise in the number, support, complexity, and increased affluency of international agricultural research centers. They have grown from four to twelve in the past six years, with a threefold increase in budget, which now (1978) approaches $100 million.[16] The United States contributes about 25 percent of the total support of these centers. They are not truly as international as is often implied, or as they should be. There is the challenge and responsibility for the LGUs and their individual scientists to build cooperative relationships in joint research programs with their counterparts in this growing network of centers. These centers, for the most part, are located in and are concentrating on food production technologies for the developing tropical countries. An equally important need is an international information service for national agricultural research centers.

"APPROPRIATE" TECHNOLOGIES

There is the issue of "labor intensive," "progressive," "capital saving," "village level," "intermediate" or "appropriate" technology in agricultural research.[17,18] "Traditional" versus "modern" agriculture is sometimes the designation. The "appropriate" technology concept attacks the large-scale, centralized, capital-energy–transport-skill intensive "hard/high" technology of modern agriculture as damaging to the environment and to human welfare, especially to the welfare of the nonaffluent, including the international poor. Conversely, "appropriate" technology focuses on labor-intensive small farms, polyculture, heterogeneous germ-plasm farming systems, little or no fertilizer or chemicals, and conservation tillage. It emphasizes the nonpolluting, decentralized inputs derived from solar energy, and is defined by its benign environmental and equitable and humanistic impacts.[21]

The United States has developed labor saving, specialized, capital, resource and management intensive large-scale food- producing systems. They are largely focused on single crop or livestock operations. This is not what the developing world needs. Projecting ahead, it may not be good for the United States.

Strategies of agricultural development for poor farmers should focus on technologies that result in stable production of conventional food crops at high levels, and on research that is scale neutral as to farm size and is non-political. Ninety-five percent of the world's food supply comes directly from plants.[19] Technologies can be labor intensive if they result in increments of production. This is true of hybrid cotton in India. Thousands of laborers are required to hand pollinate the flowers with a resulting doubling of yields.

Labor-intensive stable production at high levels, however, is not enough. There should be the least possible inputs of land, water, energy, fertilizers, and pesticides, with achievable minimal environmental inputs and improvements in nutritional quality. Such technologies can be created. We have not addressed ourselves to them because, until now, these resources have been cheap and plentiful. Food production technologies for developing countries which are sparing of water, land, energy, fertilizers, and pesticides—as well as of capital, management skills, and mechanization—have not been a part of the United States agricultural research system. Water management schemes adapted to the semiarid tropics have been given little attention. There is an ever-widening gap between irrigated and nonirrigated agriculture. This is being accompanied by increasing population pressures on the land and recurrent cycles of drought. There is a lack of technology to insure dependable harvests and to meet increased food needs.

Land, water, and energy will progressively become increasingly costly and in short supply. Technologies must be designed for their protection, conservation, and most efficient use. Agriculture is basically a solar energy processing machine. Technologies (cropping systems, pest management systems, planting designs, cultural practices, changes in plant architecture) must be sought after to maximize solar energy capture. The returns per unit land area, per unit time, and for each increment of water, energy, fertilizer, and pesticide must be increased.

HUMAN NUTRITION

One of the really surprising elements of the recently completed World Food and Nutrition Study[12] is that so little is known about human nutrition. This is especially true in ascertaining the effects of nutrition on human performance. There are also serious disease-related problems in developed countries such as the United States, as well as in low income nations. The relationships between diet, health, and performance are not known. Nor is it known how to educate and influence people in the choice, handling, and use of food. The potential role of women stands out prominently. They select and prepare most foodstuffs, and participate in crop selection. More than anyone else, they are responsible for the nutritional status, health, and well-being of people.

SMALL FARMS

Much of the rhetoric of the "Green Revolution" centers on the resulting inequalities between large and small farmers. Most all international development programs now look to the small farmer as the central figure. The small farm can be a viable economic unit. Technologies addressed to small-scale, labor intensive, capital-and-resource sparing farming would capture an unexploited food production frontier. The incomes of a billion people depend on farms of 5 hectares or less. Seventy-five percent of all farms in tropical Asia are smaller than 2 hectares. In Japan, 92 percent are 2 hectares or less. The average farm size in the Philippines is 3 hectares. Sixty-nine percent of all farms in Central America are less than 5 hectares; and the average farm size of twenty African countries is only 5.4 hectares. The output per hectare on these mini-holdings can significantly exceed that of the large United States farms. Small increments of fertilizer, water, or pesticides, or other technologies or social or economic incentives in Southeast Asia, Latin America, or Africa would have telling effects on agricultural productivity.

The issue of the small-scale or limited resource farm is not foreign to the needs of the United States. According to 1976 data, 72 percent of all United States farms gross less than $20,000 and are classified as small farms. Yet, most all United States agricultural research efforts are still directed to large-scale commercial or modern agriculture.

THE NEXT GENERATION OF AGRICULTURAL RESEARCH
This brings us to the next generation of agricultural research. Technologies are available that will result in stable food production at high levels; are nonpolluting; will add to rather than diminish the earth's resources; be sparing of capital, management, and nonrenewable resources; and are scale neutral. The time strategy, however, requires more than a three- to five-year plan. These technologies depend on mission-oriented basic research relating to the biological processes that control and now limit crop and livestock productivity. It is research that will address the problems of enabling plants and animals to more effectively utilize present environmental resources, through (1) greater photosynthetic efficiency; (2) improved biological nitrogen fixation; (3) new techniques for genetic improvement; (4) more efficient nutrient and water uptake and utilization, and reduced losses of nitrogen fertilizer from nitrification and denitrification; and (5) more resistance to competing biological systems and environmental stresses. These are the areas identified in recent National Academy of Sciences/National Research Council reports[11,12,18] and elsewhere[3,6,9,10,14,19] as grossly underfunded; where we no longer exercise world leadership, and where the United States with its vast human, financial, and natural resources could make its greatest contribution to the agricultural development of Third World nations. Such technologies would be economically, socially, and ecologically sound. They could ease the inevitable transition we must make from nonrenewable to renewable resources.

CONCLUSIONS
Agencies and organizations with conferences, symposia, workshops, seminars, and meetings are concerned with food, nutrition, agricultural research, small farmers, "appropriate" technologies, and development. International and national programs are proliferating. There is a lot of rhetoric, and reports are voluminous. Most are espoused by people who have had little, if any, farm experience. Seldom are the recommendations implemented.
Reports, speeches, and ideologies, however, do not produce food, nor deliver it to poor people who lack the purchasing power to

buy it. Only farmers produce food. Most of them are small farmers. Important ingredients for enhancement of food production by farmers are new and "appropriate" technologies. Here the opportunities are enormous that can result in improved nutrition, greater stability of supply, and an increase in production, along with the socio-economic signals to do so. Governments can, through prices, taxes, and subsidies, make or break the will of farmers to produce.

Fortunately, as T. W. Schultz has indicated,[20] plants and animals do not read reports, nor do they discriminate against ideologies, nations, or governments. One thing is certain. What people on the farm will do holds the key to the future. The most important figure in food production, the farmer, is not at all aware of the discussions that are occurring on his behalf.

The important issue is this. How will our efforts of today, yesterday, and tomorrow, including those of this special consultation, alleviate the global problems of inflation, hunger, malnutrition, poverty, unemployment, and uneven income distribution? How will they assure the future adequacy of our food supply, reduce losses in the production and handling of food, maintain a livable environment, and ease the path we must travel from the use of nonrenewable to renewable resources?   ●

INFORMAL DISCUSSION

Wittwer: There are ways in which we can add to the resources of the earth, and develop the resources, without adding increasing quantities of land, water, fertilizer, pesticides, and perhaps mechanization into the picture. This is the challenge as I see it for the future. For example:

You can go into the rice paddies of Southeast Asia, and see a green scum on the surface of the water. That green scum consists of little miniature fern known as azolla which has the capacity of fixing atmospheric nitrogen, if it's in symbiotic relationship—blue/green algae have that capability. If this relationship is optimized, it can produce about 200 pounds of nitrogen per acre per year in the rice paddies of Southeast Asia. That's valuable fertilizer.

Thirty-five percent of all that is produced in the field is never harvested because of pests—what happens in terms of insects, diseases and weeds. The most important crop on earth is rice, and 46 percent is lost there. Look at the systems of management, or the systems approach in many areas. Here's an opportunity for the future in terms of integrated pest management, putting everything together—natural enemies, chemicals, disease-resistant strains.

Interesting things come from the Chinese. The use of ducks in rice paddies to eliminate the weeds and insects—putting two food systems together. There are things we can learn from other people in terms of food production.

The water resource problem in the Punjab region of India has been met in an effective way. They have tripled grain production in ten years—the most remarkable agriculture achievement the world has known. And of course related to that are the wells, 262,000 of them, installed in that area along with other inputs. Irrigation is going to play an increasingly important role on a global scale. It can be done in terms of water management without destroying the land or water resources.

The major energy outputs in the food system go into processing and marketing. We actually spend in this nation as much energy shopping for food as producing it. Look at energy outputs and energy inputs in terms of conservation of resources. Literally thousands of methane biogas generators in South Korea are using human and animal waste to produce methane for cooking and food preparation in the home.

As you look at agricultural production you've got three major inputs: technology; the resource input of land, water, energy, fertilizer, pesticides, mechanization; and the economic incentive. You can't neglect any one of the three.

Haller: In your presentation, you imply that if we would only double, triple, or quadruple the research budgets for our land-grant institutions, that something significant would happen. I'm wondering if you also might address, related to that, the matter of quality. Is there a reformation going on within the research establishment, in the questions that are being asked and in new directions of thought?

Wittwer: I do represent an LGU, and I am a director of research. Naturally it would come out that I would be asking for dollars, because we're having a budget hearing tomorrow in the state legislature on this very topic. It's more than just dollars; the management component, the institution, has to come in. There are folk in the room here who participated in the World Food and Nutrition Study. We recommended important organizational prerequisites and changes in management of resources. What one could call science management needs to get into the picture. I am talking about somewhat new initiatives in the next generation of agriculture research. I am not talking about more land, more water, more fertilizer, or more chemicals to go into the production. There are ways in which we can increase the resources of the earth in research—photosynthetic efficiency, biological nitrogen fixation, genetic improvement. Now we're talking about both crops and livestock. We're talking about greater feed efficiency, reproductive efficiency, the means by which we enable crops and livestock to more effectively compete with other biological systems and the environment—what we call environment stresses. There are options all the way through that are not resource intensive, and would not be capital intensive, which would be in a sense scale neutral and would apply to all nations. I think we need to readdress ourselves to this.

I run an experiment station that covers eight colleges and thirty departments. The real challenge we've got ahead of us in the land-grant system is to bring disciplines together. We have that capability. It takes a different kind of administrative approach. It's administratively much more complex to bring about the solution of problems we face today than it was with the traditional problems we've dealt with. It's tough to get people together. There are many reasons why interdisciplinary research is difficult. We're going to have to look at a systems approach to problems. I mentioned pest management systems; however, we're a long way from eliminating chemicals in terms of crop production. But we're going to need to change course in the near future. On the other hand, developing countries will probably need to use more chemicals in the immediate future because you can get so much more in return for it.

We have three departments in the college of social sciences at Michigan State where we support research—anthropology, sociology, and landscape architecture and urban development. From them we get proposals relating to small-scale agriculture, it social dimensions and the economics of it—and we support them. We also support a lot of other research. I think this is one of the challenges we face in the land-grant university.

B. Baker: We hear and read that a large portion of funding for research comes from large corporations who have their own interests at stake.

Wittwer: That's ridiculous. I can tell you where our funds come from, and I can speak rather authoritatively on that one. Fifty percent of our resources come from state appropriations to the Michigan Experiment Station, another 15 percent comes from the Federal Hatch Act formula funding. The balance of 35 percent comes from public and private agencies, of which the National Science Foundation, National Institute of Health, United States Agency for International Development (USAID), National Aeronautics and Space Administration (NASA), and Energy Research and Development Agency (ERDA) play a major role. We also have major contributions in that other 35 percent from commodity groups that make contributions to research. Now that amounts to several hundred thousands of dollars if you add them all together. I would say that when it comes to large corporations and the agribusiness industry, perhaps about 3 to 5 percent comes from that source in Michigan. They do not dictate in Michigan what we do in research. We have our own research programs and our own research priorities. Now we do respond to the legislature— obviously. That's our largest granting agency. Sometimes legislatures themselves determine what we ought to be doing.

B. Baker: Do the legislators respond to large corporations?

Wittwer: It's not evident in what they do for us. I can only speak for Michigan. They will respond to vested interests, agricultural interests. For example, we had a legislator who inserted in our budget $50,000 for the support of grape research in Michigan this past year. But that's not a large corporation; that's the grape industry which is vital to the economy of the state.

G. Beran: Just within your own state have you any approximation of research funds that are spent by public entities such as yourself for agricultural development, and those that are spent by industries themselves within your state in their own research, developing agricultural chemicals and developing similar technologies and products which are then promoted?

Wittwer: That's a very good question. It's very difficult to assess what industry spends. The Agricultural Research Institute, which is a group of those that represent industry, and the state agricultural experiment station undertook a study on this a number of years ago, and it was determined that industry expends in this nation an amount about equivalent to that expended by public funds. I can't break that down for Michigan. We don't have the figures, and of course it is very difficult to get industry to respond as to what they expend in research and development.

There are some rather interesting developments when it comes to industry versus public funds support. One of the major programs of industry of course is the production of chemicals for pest control. In Michigan we have a great number of minor crops, and industry is no longer interested in doing very much about useful chemicals that would control insects, diseases, and weeds of crops produced in Michigan. If there are going to be applicable studies in this connection in terms of safety and human health and effectiveness, it will have to be increasingly more and more from public support in our state.

Killmer: Does an industry ever contract with you to do a particular piece of research? Will they come to you and say, "We're interested in X?"

Wittwer: Sometimes they come to us, yes. If there are any serious constraints about the whole business, we don't have anything to do with them. In other words, if there are restraints with respect to publication, if there are constraints we don't like with respect to license agreements, patents, we don't go that route. We have that choice.

Killmer: Has it occurred that they have just made a research grant to you for your own use?

Wittwer: Sometimes. We'll take unrestricted money from anybody (just like the church). No question about that. If it's unrestricted, that's great!

Bodine: When you were talking about the problems to solve in getting the same amount of production from the land, there's one issue I've been concerned about and I want to know if it's a real one. Namely, where I live now farmland is selling anywhere from $2500 to $3000 an acre. I imagine that's about the same where you are now.

Wittwer: It's even more than that in some places.

Bodine: As I understand how much can be produced on that land, even if the farmer were to work for nothing, he really couldn't even pay the interest on that land at that price. Economically I'm wondering where this could be leading?

Wittwer: That's quite right in terms of present prices for grain. There's no question about it; thousands of farmers are going into bankruptcy—the young farmers mostly, some older ones—and foreclosures, because the prices they receive from the land that they have and the equity that they've got in the land just don't balance out in terms of economics. Of course there were large investments made in 1973 and 1974 when prices were high, and there was a very brief period when farm prices reached parity in 1974.

Bodine: Does that mean that in the long run maybe the price of food will go up—much, much more than we are even thinking about now?

Wittwer: Traditionally we have had a cheap food policy in this nation. Constraints are an important issue when it comes to costs, constraints relating to land prices, regulatory constraints, and energy prices. And of course when you talk about energy, you talk about fertilizer, pesticides, and water. There are all kinds of interests competing for water and land and energy besides agriculture, and they are very forceful ones. Resources are going to become increasingly scarce, more competitive, more demands for them, and they will cost more. Economics has not yet distinguished between renewable and nonrenewable sources. Some day it will.

Bodine: A few years from now a loaf of bread might cost a couple of dollars or more?

Wittwer: Well, the price paid for a commodity in a supermarket does not reflect farm prices. Let's admit that. Look at the energy picture as just one example of inputs into the food system. You've got four to five times more energy going into the food system after it leaves the farm, and that energy is just one cost. There are a lot of other costs. So prices in a supermarket do not necessarily reflect what the farmer gets. The costs we encounter today are the costs of labor and costs of energy that are responsible after the product leaves the farm—the add-on cost of packaging, transportation, marketing.

Knowles: I would like to direct a few questions away from the United States. You mentioned this agricultural revolution in the Punjab and pointed out that water was involved, but I am sure that there were other factors involved. Can you identify from that example, what are the secrets, or what can be done locally, and how we can help to promote that type of development—not only there but elsewhere? And if it can be done, where do you see the church being involved?

Wittwer: I feel that the churches have not been given the credit for what they have done and can do in international development. This is not recognized by our government. (This is a statement I made to Dale Hathaway, who is assistant director in charge of International Programs in the USDA. I'd be happy to share that letter with you.)

With respect to your first question, India's great agricultural initiative in the Punjab, according to their planning commission, is in terms of irrigation. They could double the irrigated land. It's a costly route, but it could increase food production substantially and bring about a greater degree of stability. Now in terms of transplanting the system that went into the Punjab, this was essentially the transplantation of a land-grant system in the Punjab state of India. They developed tube wells. (Water in the Punjab is a renewable resource with no problems of salinity as they use it.) The initiative worked very well for a number of reasons, and I think we need to analyze that. When we were there I asked some of the Punjabi people that very question—but that's rather complex. We don't have time to go into detail right now. But there are examples where the land-grant system has worked abroad, and that's one of them. They had the production efficiency and the resources to build upon. Another example of agricultural initative you see in the Gujerat state of India is known as the White Revolution. A graduate of a land-grant school went there and organized dairy cooperatives. All over the Gujerat state millions of farmers deliver milk twice a day for cash, which substantially alleviates poverty, provides employment and a cash income, and improves nutrition. Now you can pick those isolated segments out in various parts of the world, and I think a very fascinating thing to do would be to look at the ingredients that make them successful. The problem is the ingredients of success are very localized, very provincial, and there's no one solution that you can replicate and apply to other parts of the world. Have I evaded the question?

Knowles: It just seems to me that while it may be difficult maybe the church could analyze the ingredients of success and identify to what extent it is transferable to other places.

Wittwer: If I were to give a formula in terms of success for agricultural development abroad, I would come out with: agricultural technologies that are labor intensive that would result in stable production at high levels which are scale neutral and which would have a minimum of capital, management, and resource inputs. That would be my formula. I can give you examples of those very things. We just haven't addressed ourselves to developing those kinds of technologies extensively, and I'm saying that's a challenge for the LGUs—to look at labor intensive, high-producing technologies resulting in stable production, scale neutral, that will optimize crop and livestock utilization of the environments that exist, be sparing of capital, management, and resources. That's initiative in terms of all of us. That applies to the churches and the LGUs.

Another area for innovation is storage of indigenous production. That is something we ought to get with. And it doesn't take high, hard technology. It's a social problem and also a little technical problem.

Lundy: Can you speak in more detail to the reasons for responding to the challenge? A lot of citizens and a lot of legislators ask why American LGUs are getting involved with that? That's not a need in Illinois or Michigan!

Wittwer: Excellent point, and some of you are going to talk about "Title XII" of the International Development Act. Of course it may be titled something else before it's revised by Congress because Hubert Humphrey's last venture was to get this whole package of foreign assistance into a different kind of formula.

Yes, we are involved internationally. During 1977 the United States shipped abroad $25 billion worth of agricultural commodities. You can't escape from the international dimension as far as the LGUs in this nation are concerned. We ship abroad 25 percent of the navy beans we produce in Michigan. We've got to educate our legislators in Congress. They need to be informed, as we are informed, that we do have an international commitment, by act of Congress, and we're going to have to rethink how we manage and conduct international agricultural research. We need to remember also that there are benefits which we need to convey to the legislators. We likewise can benefit by international involvement in the research and development area. We can learn from them as well as we can do things for them. We've a lot of things we've already "picked up" in international development. This is an educational process. It's a very good question. We haven't done very well in putting this message across.

Hadwiger: Assume that there are a number of groups—church groups and others—that could provide considerable support, or increased funding for agricultural research, but that they want to support the kinds of things you were talking about because they don't have confidence across-the-board in research leadership. They worry that if we go for more funding, appropriate agricultural research may not necessarily be done. What kinds of research mechanisms could they use or should they insist on, if any, to get that kind of mission commitment?

Wittwer: If you're going to change the establishment, you have to get the actors involved in the changes. Of course I refer now to the so-called land-grant establishment. You're not going to go into the land-grant institution and enact changes from the outside; you're going to have to have the actors themselves involved in this. We found that out in the World Nutrition Study; you've got to get the agencies and the representatives involved. We need to deal directly with the people we expect to implement our recommendations. We must build upon the strengths we have and then get the involvement of the people who will be engaged in the act; namely, defuse the resistance at the outset. I'm serious; we have to participate. You don't just throw something at the land-grant school and say, "Do this."

McKenzie: Could we add to that the difficulty, if not the impossibility, of ever identifying in advance the kind of research that would produce the results you want? There is almost no way that folks can be charted far enough down the road to produce the type of research you suggest.

Wittwer: Unfortunately, you can't predict the results of research. If you could, you wouldn't do the research.

Hadwiger: You can predict the results of a lot of highly applied research. . . .

Wittwer: Problem solving. Yes, if you've got a problem and you utilize sufficient resources to solve it, it is likely you're going to solve the problem.

Stockdale: As a matter of fact that's what we've been doing for years.

B. Baker: Does your comment about low energy use in terms of production methods also apply to this country?

Wittwer: Well, there are trade-offs, and I think these have to be examined very carefully. We all know the constraints that are coming forth in terms of availability, in terms of a nonrenewable resource, in terms of costs, and my message before any audience I can get to listen to me is that one-third of all energy going into agricultural production is in nitrogen fertilizer, not mechanization.

B. Baker: Are you doing research in that area?

Wittwer: We're trying to push it, and at Michigan State we've taken on three new people in this area.

J. Conner: You commented about the lack of increase in numbers of researchers in the last decade. What's the reason for this?

Wittwer: Agriculture, up until recently in this nation, has been characterized by surpluses and low prices. You go to legislators and they say, "What do you want more research for? More production? We've got too much now, and we're already subsidizing research." The real thing with respect to LGUs, and this is the focus of this conference, is that there's been a threefold increase in enrollment in thirteen years. (Incidentally, the enrollment of women has doubled since 1973.) Now we have the same faculty, the same number of teachers— no increase there. What has happened is that in the LGU you have dual appointments: teaching, extension, and research. Many of our professors do all three. Many of our professors are halftime teachers, halftime researchers. Well, you can imagine what happens to research when enrollment triples. Research is a remnant left behind. There's little time for research. Also the same thing is true with respect to equipment, space, and facilities. They're jointly used. If you've got the students there, you've got to take care of them. They come first. We're always told in the LGU "Teaching comes first."

One other point that you need to remember with respect to the land-grant system and a total research component is that there has been no federal input in terms of new facilities or new equipment for twelve years. We're using the same facilities and equipment that we did twelve years ago, and we've got problems. We've got problems at home even before we make commitments in terms of international development—we can't take care of the home problems. The most important resource in the land-grant system is the human resource, and that has been eroded.

J. Conner: The church in concert with the land-grant school should see its role in supporting appropriate kinds of research that, as you indicate, cannot be pulled off at this point because of lack of public interest and subsidy.

Wittwer: Excellent point. Let me mention one more, which concerns the present administration. In spite of all our efforts in the Food and Agricultural Act of 1977, which some of us had a hand in bringing about and which was the result of the combined effort of three different committees in Congress (the House Agricultural Committee, the House Committee on Science and Technology, and the Senate Committee on Agriculture), the Food and Agricultural Act of 1977 called for major increases in certain kinds of agriculture research—funding, special competitive grants programs, and increased research in human nutrition. There has been a $50 million increase in competitive grants with a concurrent decrease in Hatch formula funding, the very base by which the LGU system has survived. It doesn't make sense. A messsage has to get through to somebody. We thought we had gotten the message through. We have to start all over now. The resource base, the financial base of the land-grant system in extension, in research, in teaching, is being grossly eroded in this year's fiscal budget as it came out of the White House. Congress can perhaps do something about this, and Congress is becoming increasingly more effective.

J. Conner: Isn't that a result of the conclusion that the university exists directly for the consumer, rather than for the common good of the society?

Wittwer: I don't see how we can continue to separate the two.

4 ACHIEVING AGRICULTURAL RESEARCH MISSIONS

DON F. HADWIGER

THE HAWTHORNE EFFECT is getting a new test in food research, and it is likely to fail. In the famous Hawthorne "efficiency" study it was discovered that if you give attention to the workers, they will achieve more, regardless how you change (or don't change) the other conditions of their work.

Agricultural scientists have received much praise recently for having increased the world's food supply and much criticism for the way they did it. Now there are expectations that agricultural science will produce more miracles and do so in more acceptable packages than in the past.

The agricultural universities have been making a quiet revolution for years in a setting of conventional campus communities. Agricultural science has transformed food and its production. It has made the family farm perhaps irrevocably obsolete by introducing new strains of capital- and energy-intensive farming. The vast arsenal of technology developed primarily at the land-grant universities has provided the means for historic advances in agricultural "productivity" and "efficiency."

However, as production has increased, so has criticism. A nascent consumer movement has begun to ask whether, for all the visual changes in our food, it is any safer or more nutritious than it was. Others have noted that while the Green Revolution has kept supplies of rice and wheat rising with the world's population, more and more of the food supply finds its way to the bellies of the affluent. Still others have wondered if corporate agriculture, combining maximum productivity with minimum employment, can be adapted to those poorer nations where what is needed is both more food and more jobs.

THE AGRICULTURAL RESEARCH ESTABLISHMENT

Agricultural scientists, who live in a subculture with its own reward structure, seem uncomfortable in the presence of new ex-

Don H. Hadwiger is professor of political science at Iowa State University, Ames, Iowa.

pectations from outsiders. It is taken for granted that they will continually find ways to increase food supplies, and they are now expected to develop "appropriate technology" for labor-surplus countries and to find production techniques more protective of the soil, the environment, and food consumers.

These demands come at a moment when the research establishment needs renewal, more than new tasks. Earlier scientific breakthroughs such as hybridization have been exploited, while promising ideas such as manipulation of DNA are not yet practical.

Furthermore, existing technology is faltering. Irrigated soils are becoming salty. Water and energy—the foundation stones of current abundance—are being depleted or diverted to other uses. Farmers are abandoning longtime soil conservation practices. And pesticides no longer work well against some major insects.

Should big agriculture—which has provided our ample food and our major exports—be encouraged to expect researchers to concoct ever more precarious technologies—for example, creating pockmarks of fertile soil on lands otherwise choked with salt? Red flags are being dropped by environmentalists and other new interests, who demand an end to desperate interventionist strategies. The further development of agricultural research may depend upon support (rather than opposition) from these interests. This support has been forthcoming, but with some concern as to whether the scientists and research administrators who have been so committed to "efficiency at any price" can actually be turned around.

The researchers themselves are in an "old-age" cycle, and while there is an abundance of young talent within some scientific fields, in other fields too few new researchers have been trained.

For their part, the agricultural scientists enjoy the attention they are getting, but they are apprehensive and even gloomy about the gap they observe between their capacity and our new expectations. They are becoming angry because, in their view, "society" asks them to solve the food problem in new ways but spends its money on food stamps.

Both more money and new directions for research are needed. Both were promised in a new research charter passed by Congress as part of the 1977 farm bill, but those who made these legislative promises were not immediately able to deliver the funds, as illustrated by the reduced research budgets and personnel allotments for 1978 and 1979.

The new research law is the product of the increased attention given to the missions and to the management of agricultural research. The larger scientific community has conducted several separate studies, including the recent National Academy of Science Study authorized by the White House, undertaken by more than a dozen teams of eminent scientists. In Congress, both the Office of Technology Assessment and the House Committee on Science and Technology have produced major reviews of agricultural research, and the congressional agricultural committees finally took responsibility for oversight of agricultural research. Within the federal research bureaucracy, planning structures were created which require the full-time efforts of more than a hundred scientists.

The research establishment has been honored by the caliber of its recent critics, if not by what they say—including Rachel Carson, *Science* magazine, Jim Hightower, and now the United Farm Workers. A myriad of grass roots organizations throughout the land are now keenly interested in agricultural technology. Unfortunately, there has been more interest in giving advice to the research establishment than in learning what its insights and needs may be, or what motivates it to do good work.

Agricultural research is part of an agricultural subculture. Susan DeMarco who (with Jim Hightower and Susan Sechler) looked critically at researchers within the agricultural subsystem, said she started out looking for a conspiracy of big business and big farmers that could explain why agricultural research was, in her judgment, grossly misdirected. Instead of a conspiracy, she found a network of "good old boys" who knew each other from "back when;" who had journeyed together, even as they went into different institutions, and sometimes back and forth to corporations, universities, and public service.

It is a worldwide fraternity. My institution, Iowa State University, recently held a world food conference which assembled scientists from many countries. At the conference it became evident that under the turbans and saris, and behind the many-shaped faces, were many scientists of the good-old-boys and -girls circuit from Cornell, Purdue, and Iowa State.

INSIDE THE SUBCULTURE

Public agricultural research is conducted by federal research agencies (mostly within the USDA) and at state LGUs, both of which receive federal funding. Agricultural research is conducted primarily at fifty-five state agricultural experiment stations. These research agencies are located within the colleges of agriculture at the LGUs, where research is interwoven with the training of new agricultural scientists. The land-grant colleges were founded under the

Morrill Act of 1862 with the express purpose of teaching better farming practices. The "experiment stations" or research arms were created under the Hatch Act of 1887, but today receive only about a quarter of their funds from the federal government, with the rest coming from the states and private sources. There are, in addition, six research agencies with the USDA, a large proportion of whose scientists are stationed on university campuses. And agribusiness corporations, while developing brand products in their own laboratories, receive considerable assistance from the publicly subsidized researchers.

Agricultural research is a highly decentralized activity. Individual researchers or teams of researchers receive funds for projects with rather vague titles that would presumably allow researchers some degree of freedom. But in fact, the mission of the research institutions is quite constrained. They have been integrated into a social and political system that has shaped their growth and function and determined the careers and values of the researchers. As a result, the agricultural colleges have departed considerably from the original purpose of providing research and education for small farmers.

The two research systems operate in the same subculture and their scientists usually cooperate closely, but they are nevertheless competing for funds under rather static (and surprisingly small) federal-state research budgets. And the competition is provoking some bitterness. One agricultural scientist in the USDA remarked to me, "He's one of them," referring to his political boss Rupert Cutler, the Assistant Secretary of Agriculture for Conservation and Research. By "them" I first assumed he meant the outside critics: the conservationists (Cutler was once editor of the *National Wildlife Federation Newsletter*); the environmentalists; the organic farmers; and the consumer advocates. These particular outsiders have intensely shared values and experiences and so might be entitled to be called "them." But no, this scientist was referring to "them" in the state-level agricultural research establishment. (Cutler was previously an associate professor at Michigan State University.)

Consider the backgrounds of this era's agricultural researchers. Most were raised in farming areas that either were one-party Republican or Southern Democratic, and as professionals they have remained under the sponsorship of conservative politicans from these areas. They went to "cow colleges," so named by others who thereby failed to credit these institutions for their good science and useful achievements. Like other "second-class citizens," these scientists developed their own status and reward structure, which incorporated the work ethic and the success ethic, taught from 4-H to Ph.D.

Their work ethic was also an efficiency ethic. It was the legislative mandate of agricultural research to become a practical science—helping farmers use their long workdays to gain more output and a better living standard. These researchers became particularly eager to save farmers from such manual tasks as scooping, hoeing, picking, and milking. The scientists, earlier as farm kids, had been obliged to perform these tasks which place men so romantically close to nature, and they had found them painful. They had observed that others also preferred to escape such work. And the farmers found, as John Brewster noted, that when researchers had to choose between equalitarian values and individual success, they went with the success-oriented farmers because, as practical scientists, their first task was to find a "user."

In striving to be useful, scientists quickly accepted the truth that ours is a capitalist society. As the food economy moved off the farm into implement companies, chemical companies, and food processing and marketing corporations, the scientists followed the action. I once wrote that they had become "hired hands of agribusiness," and indeed they were anxious to be helpful and not to displease, in order to get a user and some research money. I now think that they were, on the whole, a disturbingly innovative presence within industries and bureaucracies that would have preferred to change slowly or not at all.

As a result, agriculture, which elsewhere is a "backward" industry, in this country became one of the most efficient industries. For more than a decade stable United States food prices moderated national inflation, and food products—both raw and processed—were preeminent items that the United States was able to sell abroad. But the pursuit of efficiency proved to be poor political strategy, and even poor economics when the cheap resources on which it relied were no longer cheap. Abundant food did not result in support for increased research budgets from producers who faced "surpluses," or from congress and the president who spent money to solve problems rather than to reward achievements.

FROM CRITICISM TO COALITION

However, once the research establishment lost its sacred cow status, its response to critics—outraged and also condescending—helped the critics make their main point: the research establishment was indifferent to the side effects of its "success." Paradoxically the critics in turn boosted the establishment—by convincing politicians that research was indeed a "problem" area, and by broadening support for research far beyond the impotent agricultural establishment.

It was this coalition of critics and establishment which enacted the 1977 promise of increased funding. These confusing events can be explained.

I do not doubt that the research establishment had ignored environmental costs. It had also ignored costs to displaced workers and declining rural communities, health hazards from food additives, soil losses, effects on human nutrition, and the skewing of research benefits to better-off consumers. It was expedient to ignore these things, because the producers and the agribusiness interests which supported research funding did not want to bear these costs, and therefore did not want to hear about them; on that matter they were brutally dictatorial.

This is illustrated by research on human nutrition. After a brilliant beginning within the United States agricultural research establishment, nutrition research became a "hot potato" in the 1940s when the USDA's planning agency persisted in suggesting that farm programs should seek nutritional goals ahead of farm income goals. Angry rural congressmen abolished that planning agency, and for twenty-five years nutrition research languished. As of now, we do not know whether our processed foods, which come from many soils, are more nutritious, or less nutritious, than those from the family garden. We do not know enough about what the human body needs, and what we do know has not been effectively disseminated, for fear of producer reaction.

Critics who wanted to put nutrition and other problems on the agenda undertook through a media campaign to build an interested public which could end producer and agribusiness monopoly over research decisions. They proceeded by two steps: first, to establish a "crisis" perspective; and second, to prove that the establishment was grossly negligent. Rachel Carson's 1962 book *Silent Spring* described the insidious spread of enduring poisons—pesticides—which were exterminating our birds and which would kill some of us too. *Hunger USA,* a 1969 document by civil rights groups, revealed widespread malnutrition and occasional starvation in America. Television documentaries explored the deformed bodies of malnourished children, living outside the fence rows of an abundant agriculture. Friendly congressional committees found an establishment indifferent to this shame, and the establishment's response confirmed its negligence.

The establishment's first defense was: "The critics lack scholarly or expert credentials." But who cared, if the facts spoke for themselves? The second defense was: "The critics are self-interested—seeking profit through notoriety." But the defenders had reaped large material rewards. The third defense was: "This is not a crisis, only a longstanding problem of which we are fully aware." But most crises are mental constructs, occurring when a problem becomes widely perceived to be serious, whether or not it is longstanding; and those activated by a crisis are mostly on the side of the people who brought it to their attention. Thus, the defense of the establishment was reassuring only to the establishment, and it made establishment leaders seem narrow minded as well as politically inept.

Critics of the establishment took control of the farm policy agenda, and with help from friendly congressmen and committees, they expanded the food and nutrition programs (which were allotted more than half of the total USDA budget). They reformed pesticide laws and removed pesticide regulation from the USDA. They achieved other subtle changes of direction, although there are still many items on the "new agenda" in research and action programs which have yet to be fully addressed.

From this conflict between the agricultural establishment and the advocates of a new agenda, a coalition emerged. In Congress this coalition easily passed a many-faceted 1977 farm bill, which authorized research on small farm alternatives, on solar energy, and on basic research designed to foster new strategies for maintaining high productivity but with less heroic (and less disastrous) challenges to the natural ecological system.

In the Carter Administration, the new food politics coalition was implanted within the USDA, whose assistant secretaries were drawn not from commercial farming but from active careers concerned with rural poverty, consumer protection, wildlife conservation, and international development. Wildlife conservationist Rupert Cutler was placed in charge of agricultural research, and he and other USDA leaders have spent much time seeking outside and inside support for new research missions.

They have not been very successful at the presidential level. Agricultural research is not one of the large, squeaky wheels which preoccupy the President. Nor does it fit well into the full employment, less inflation mission of the President's Council of Economic Advisers, or that of the Office of Management and Budget (OMB), whose job is to reduce personnel and funding in all "controllable" areas such as agricultural research. In the 1978 budget, the OMB offered sizeable increases for nutrition research and basic research while continuing the practice of recent years of sharply cutting the overall research budget.

So one major task of the new food coalition, having gained authorization for increased research funding, is to get that money appropriated. The coalition is one of many supplicants to OMB, and its success depends on several things: the degree to which new groups can continue to expand public interest in food research; how strongly it can argue that declining agricultural research is a national and international problem; and the credibility of its claim that the research establishment is actually ready to pursue new missions.

Its credibility is heavily damaged by the congressional appropriations process, where an embittered House subcommittee chairman, Jamie Whitten, once the most influential figure in the agricultural establishment, has preferred to let his power erode rather than practice new-coalition politics. In 1977, Whitten slashed funding for new missions that had been added by OMB, while permitting large increases of funding for pet projects of congressional colleagues.

And Whitten has continued to demand fealty from research bureaucrats—a fealty ingrained by decades of political cooperation and by shared ideological outlooks, but which administrators now reluctantly perceive to be a source of their difficulties with OMB and with the new coalition which authorized their increased funding. The appropriations committees are probably not an enduring roadblock; majority members in both houses are now liberal on balance, and for the first time, they are not letting House Chairman Whitten make all the decisions. It is to be hoped that critics of agricultural research, though now a part of the new coalition, will continue to point up its omissions in a forceful way that expands public support, and obliges the research establishment to devote resources to these new missions. Agricultural scientists now bless critic Rachel Carson, whose book yielded them laboratories for studying alternative pest controls; and undoubtedly they will bless those who can find a way to persuade the OMB to fund the new legislative mandates.

At the same time, the research establishment is unlikely to abandon its heavy commitment to commercial agriculture; nor should it actually be abandoned, because this system is the source of our abundant food and agricultural exports. But just as the scientists have always endured high-handed and bossy commodity groups, they are learning to live with the critics who challenge their biases toward large and often inefficient producers who neglect the soil, the environment, and the health of consumers.

NEW RESEARCH MISSIONS

The means are also being found to persuade the research establishment to address the new research missions. One of these is the development of research centers (centers for human nutrition research embody a permanent commitment). Another is "competitive grants" for specific missions, as an alternative to simply giving more money to the establishment. Competitive grants were recommended in the President's National Academy of Science study, by the congressional Office of Technology Assessment, and by the House Committee on Science and Technology, and they became an important vehicle for new research funding in the 1977 farm bill. Scientists—in the public research agencies and outside them—must compete for these funds, which are influential because they provide the increment to institutional funding that sets directions. The same is true of "extramural" grants from such federal and state action agencies as the Environmental Protection Agency and the Department of Energy which have been stimulants for research on the use of sewage sludge as fertilizer, and on developing solar energy uses in agriculture. The competitive and extramural grants are a way to secure mission orientation without splitting up the research establishments into mission-oriented segments that cannot do the basic or fundamental research that is applicable to many missions.

Agricultural scientists themselves harbor many humane concerns, prompted by their proximity to the soil and the ecosystem, and some of these concerns go beyond those of their critics. Soil scientists know we are losing the struggle to save the soil—the abandonment of crop rotation, the use of big machinery which rips out the terraces built over the decades by federal subsidies, the extensive use of fertilizer to compensate for depleted soil, the row-cropping of steep hillsides, and the destruction of shelter belts. Soil scientists would like to develop a new set of conservation practices (not to mention a new set of farmer incentives) that would reduce the massive soil losses and the resulting pollution of waterways.

Equally reckless, in their view, is the waste of nonrenewable water resources through inefficient irrigation systems, and the progressive salinization of soil that immediately threatens California's Imperial Valley as well as other irrigated lands which now produce a large proportion of our fresh food supply.

Pest control is an area of mutual concern. Despite talk and even official promises about "eradicating" the boll weevil and other major pests, we may in fact be losing the capacity to control these pests which are becoming immune to pesticides. Meanwhile the "non-chemical" solutions once advocated by Rachel Carson are not yet fully effective or are themselves potentially dangerous. For example, plants can be made insect-resistant by breeding in toxins, but these plants may turn out to be poisonous also to the animals and humans who consume them.

Scientists are reacting rather quickly to the increased costs of fertilizer and fuel. Sooner than might have been expected, they are retreating from total commitment to large-scale agriculture. Until this year, "organic farming" was a dirty word, but the costs and the frequent ineffectiveness of synthetic chemicals are changing that view.

Critics of agricultural research, it is hoped, will continue to point up its omissions in a forceful way that expands public concern. Despite the off and on "food crisis," it is difficult to focus attention upon complex, future-oriented research programs. Agricultural scientists undoubtedly will bless those who can find a way to persuade the OMB and state governments to fund the new legislative mandates.

A PUBLIC AGENDA

Here are some of the questions we should be asking agricultural scientists and administrators:

1. How are you moving to integrate the earlier research to perfect largely organic agriculture with the new environment in which inorganic fertilizer has become more expensive and in which pesticides have become less effective and less acceptable? In what ways are you cooperating with organic farmers who are willing to use their farms and ideas for experimentation? And what are you doing to help farmers bring about a reconciliation of these farming strategies?

2. To what extent is your research promoting as economically feasible strategies that destroy natural resources: such as irrigating arid lands with water that pollutes the soil, or ground water (from aquifers) which is not being replaced; such as the application of inorganic fertilizers to compensate for erosion or destruction of top soil?

3. To what extent are research priorities gauged to improve human nutrition rather than to make a profit?

4. To what extent is research designed to suit the convenience of farmers and input manufacturers under current technologies, rather than being designed to develop technologies which conserve the natural environment and protect the soil: for example, are there entomology departments which devote most of their research and extension resources to the testing of new brands of pesticides?

In short, to what extent has agricultural research become devoted to a strategy of desperation—for the first time in its existence being devoted to preserving bankrupt technologies rather than being devoted to the hopeful assumption that this generation can produce technologies which do not destroy natural resources in order to produce current abundance?

Questions such as these were asked by Rachel Carson, Jim Hightower, and others. They are basically constructive questions, usually framed in rather dramatic ways in order to gain support from an interested public and from policymakers. The first round of critics has made an impact. We must continue to ask these questions, perhaps on the basis of better information and in a manner sympathetic to the realities of current farming and current food needs. Researchers are attentive to this perspective, but they still lack the resources and the will to embrace it as they have embraced the development of current technologies.

We should also be asking the question: Who should farm? Farming is an activity to aid people—both those who consume the food and those whose livelihood depends on it. In this country, we have largely displaced hard labor in agriculture, to some extent for the wrong reasons such as to avoid having to deal with unskilled workers—and their unions. Nevertheless the new technology has created new jobs that most people in fact prefer over the old tasks of hand-milking cows, handpicking cotton, and hand-weeding crops. Yet in some situations, particularly in developing countries, it appears that labor-intensive technologies are preferable—because they are more environmentally sound, because people have no current alternatives for employment, and because these practices can be more productive. Technologies for labor-intensive agriculture must have a high priority on campuses that train many of the world's agricultural scientists, and which are a principal source of new technology.

What, specifically, should be done? First, we should find out what is going on at our research institutions. We can do this by requesting, and reading, the Current Research Information System (CRIS) project reports, which should be available to all seriously interested citizens (perhaps at some small cost) from the USDA. These reports describe the projects of all scientists receiving funding through USDA and other public institutions.

Then, with appreciation for the complexity of the subject matter, we should feel free to have informal discussions and seminars with the people doing the research and their administrators. The researchers and administrators are usually in communication with commercial producers and with the agribusiness industry in order to find users, to obtain supplementary private funding, and to develop political support. Thus researchers are already committed to talking with people who have ideas and can provide support for them. Those who express public concerns are surely as legitimate as those who plead their private interests.

Second, we should also support funding for long-range strategies that serve humans, natural resources, and the physical environment; or that seek to perceive and serve the interests of future generations. To the extent that researchers and administrators are slow to devote institutional resources to these purposes, funding must be made conditional upon their doing so—"competitive grants" for specific research purposes, "extramural funding" controlled by agencies whose missions are to improve human resources and the environment, the establishment of "centers" for soil conservation and human nutrition research, and commensurate reductions in institutional funding. These are in a sense harsh measures because, while they provide research direction, they also presume an inadequate perspective on the part of the research establishment.

At the same time, it is hard to imagine that a research establishment can live hand-to-mouth, off of mission-oriented competitive grants. The research establishment has many basic tasks: it must train the next generation of researchers; it must do fundamental research; it must preserve the genetic materials; it must maintain a communication system; and it must develop its will, its pride, and its sense of urgency in performing its vital missions. So even as it may need outside direction, it also needs strong political support for its legitimate institutional needs. And it deserves our appreciation. ●

INFORMAL DISCUSSION

Hadwiger: First, a brief summary of the political situation. I offer this postulation on the basis of considerable study, without having reached a strong conclusion. Today there are three coalitions concerned with agricultural research at the federal level.

1. One of these is the old agricultural establishment, made up of commodity producers, the USDA agencies, and the land-grant institutions. These groups, knitted together over time, made exclusive decisions for many years on all aspects of agriculture. That group, in my opinion, still holds sway in the House Appropriations Committee. The overall membership of that committee has changed. It is urban, new-mission oriented, noncommodity-oriented, and it is at least as liberal as Congress as a whole, though not as liberal as the Senate committee. What you have in that committee at the present time, however, is a preeminent chairman (since 1949), Congressman Whitten—a most knowledgeable person and a person most interested in agriculture research—who runs the subcommittee. That committee's power has eroded. Lately have they done a good job for agricultural research? The answer is no, they couldn't come through. They did raise the budget bureau's figure, but that's of minor

significance, because the budget bureau has been cutting back as much as 20 percent each year. Ken Meier, a political scientist at Rice University, did a careful study of organizational lobbying before these appropriations committees throughout the federal government. He asked, "Who did the best job? And what do you know?" One of the ten best agencies was the Agricultural Research Service, the federal research agency in the USDA. It had the most witnesses testifying for it, it had the best organized witnesses, and it had the best cross section. Terrific! Later in his paper he says: "Wow, what a powerful, political organization." And then he looks at their budget, and their funding, and he says: "What went wrong?" I think the answer is that the coalition is impotent, relative to the others that are around today. Food stamps must have depended on something else.

2. The second coalition is a combination of new groups, lots of them, with different kinds of strategies. They are environmentally concerned; some of them are very old conservationist groups—and some of them are very new. They are interested in small farms. There is a large organic-farming movement today, and it is getting more politically adept. Some of them, like Bread for the World, are interested in feeding people at home and abroad. Bread for the World is very well organized. It's got a lot of people in different districts, and they use certain techniques. They've been able to use the media very effectively, and the agricultural establishment has reacted in such a way as to reinforce their strength.

That coalition of new groups expanded the conflict. They brought into this interest in agricultural research an enormous new constituency. It was a conflict constituency to start with. It was Jim Hightower and Susan DeMarco. Where are those people today? Those people passed the 1977 farm bill in a joint coalition with the agricultural subsystem, with that old establishment, but with certain leadership in that establishment; those groups were represented in the House Agriculture Committee; they were represented on the Committee for Science and Technology that Sylvan Wittwer was talking about; they were represented in the Office of Technology Assessment. All over the place these groups were present. The solar energy bill was written by Peggy Wheeler, who is in her mid-twenties. She wrote pages of the legislation. She had an ad hoc coalition for energy in the House. The result was that the research provisions of the bill, as well as the bill itself, went through without dissent. The research provision, which is very large and which increases enormously agricultural research by authorization, went through without dissent and with great compliments all around. Not that everybody liked everything, but they made a successful coalition.

3. What's the other coalition? It is the Executive Branch Coalition (White House is one way to put it), but there are also institutions in the White House like the Council of Economic Advisers, the OMB, and there are interdepartmental committees. And if you look at the number of different agencies that have participated in agricultural decision-making in the Executive branch, it's gone down and down, and you've got, finally, a list of about twenty agencies that are doing agricultural policymaking. Obviously, in the case of the department heads, they have their own interests, and the Secretary of Agriculture who sits on those committees has only one vote. In the OMB, they don't have a lot of expertise; only one person looks at agricultural research. This holds true for the Council of Economic Advisers, with only one person. This is not to say that they are uninformed. The World Food and Nutrition Study was read carefully by both of those persons, and they claim that was the major reason for the $50 million increase in competitive research. They actually suggested a 1978 budget of $28 million, and Congressman Whitten cut it down to $10 million, but they did know something about funding for research. They talked with consumer groups, something relatively new, and they listened to public-interest groups.

So those are the three coalitions. The White House isn't basically interested in agricultural research. It's interested in some big crises that face the nation now, some very large, squeaky wheels which are not agricultural. Agriculture is a success story; agriculture is something to be used and manipulated. It's not something you have to give money to, and so they have a certain level of information. It's outside information, and it's to some degree critical. They need a very strong push if they are to give small increases of money to research for technical development or research for any of these new missions. They need a strong push, even though they're friendly toward it. When they do give something more, they give it for those reasons. I'm arguing that this combination of coalitions can provide what amounts to relatively small but very adequate increments in the national budget. And there are ways that those funds can be committed to the kinds of research missions that we are talking about here.

Let me say one more thing. I think that one can look at CRIS reports of federally supported research projects on your campus and not be knowledgeable enough to make conclusions about them. But one can go and talk with department heads and scientists on the campus and say, "We're interested in these areas. Does your research explore these areas? What kinds of research would you really like to do in these areas, if you could? Maybe we can support that kind of research, or maybe we can support research institutionally in a more general way.'' Take a positive approach, and I think you'll find that agricultural scientists are humane people. They have some concerns that haven't been raised yet, such as natural resource conservation. They care a whole lot more about that than the new-agenda groups do. Who's talking about soil conservation? Well, you go to your agronomy chairman—that's who's talking about soil conservation today.

The other thing that would help is sensitivity training. Sometimes we disdain it saying: ''Who needs sensitivity training, it's just a GI exercise.'' I don't think so. The USDA used sensitivity training to promote civil rights, and they moved peoples' attitudes by many degrees. It was just one of the things they did. I know at this university, campus ministers and other people have been practicing sensitivity training for years, and I suspect it's a lot more effective than we know because it just proliferates. I think that's another thing that can be done.

Killmer: That was a fascinating description of the politics. I'm interested in the other half of the politics which you didn't talk much about. Research administrators have quite a bit of power over how that research money is spent. Are the same [three] coalitions at work helping to influence how that money is spent in particular agencies and at particular campuses, and if not, is the first group you described—the old line establishment—really in control of how funds are spent?

Hadwiger: I know a little bit about Iowa. I did a study of pesticides. In Iowa there are no new-agenda forces to speak of. I'm sure church groups have had some impact. Churches are organized, both Protestant and Catholic federations, but mostly their concern is with social welfare. What happened in pesticides was that some farmers were very concerned about what goes into rivers and tried to work out a bill that would prevent the abuse of pesticides, but not the use of them. In short, the answer is no. There's no new-agenda coalition yet at the state level. There's no reason why there couldn't be. One example of the possibilities of the governor's role in agricultural research is that of Governor Jerry Brown of California. He has taken a fairly strong hand, at least symbolically, with respect to a new agenda of agricultural research. In California there is a conflict situation. It seems to me that they have not achieved a coalition as yet. Keep in mind that federal research tends to do a lot, and that it can provide an increment. If you take a competitive grant and put it on top of an institutional grant, even though it is much smaller, it will establish the direction.

Killmer: Therefore, if people are interested in stimulating research or the kinds of concerns we've been talking about, their concern has to be addressed not only to Washington, but to the governor of the state, the state legislature, and to the Sylvan Wittwers of this world who also have some control over how those funds are spent.

Hadwiger: Right. The Mr. Wittwers of this world (and he's unusually progressive) have control over the new people coming in. That's their basic control. They have a 10 percent turnover of personnel every year. And they decide where that new 10 percent will go.

Watts: I'd like to add just a little bit to your question. I think that the add-on monies that come from Washington that are descriptive of a new thrust can then be identified as that thrust is implemented, whether it's in research or extension. As far as the decisions in terms of program go, I think your [Hadwiger's] comment was correct; the most critical decisions are made at the state level unless they involve new initiatives with specific money behind them. Why? Because any institution is composed in large measure of tenured faculty who cannot be transferred from the agronomy department to the political science department by an act of an administrator, or if they do, they don't function too well. What we're searching for, I think, is the team work by which the agronomist, political scientist, along with an entomologist, and let's say a range ecologist, may develop some common thrust.

But we need to take a look at these dollars that are supposedly allocated for research—what happens is often confusing. For example, this year in Title 14 of the farm bill there's authorization for a lot of new research money, but it isn't in the appropriations. In terms of the program thrusts of the USDA this year, most of the departments [Forest Service, experiment stations, the Agricultural Research Service (ARS)], are being cut, and there's a $6 million increase in the secretaries' offices. What is going on? There's a movement in Washington (and this started before the current administration) designed to make the public feel that we're going to put a ceiling on the agencies, and that we'll cap these positions and cut them down by 10, 15, or 20 percent. Is this designed to save money for the taxpayer? No. The dollars were cut; all it does is take a given program and reduce the people that can perform in the job mandated by the legislation. They've got some money floating around in the departments that they really can't administer effectively, because they haven't got a full complement of people. And so a lot of strange things are done that you should be aware of if you're not inside the land-grant system.

Your question does indicate that when you get right down to the nitty-gritty, the state is the most critical decision-making point. I think it's true in extension as well as in any research establishment.

Hadwiger: I agree with you. What you are talking about then is a declining budgetary situation that causes restrictions on the use of the department's monies and reduces flexibility in the short term. In that sense, it is a constraint on the decision capacity at the state level.

Watts: It's more restrictive than it appears.

Hadwiger: Right. Without the institutional funding to go along with directed grants, you don't have the personnel and the education to follow through.

Watts: I know in the Colorado legislature, particularly with research, they have fussed: "Don't you ever terminate research projects and start something new?" The experiment director has spent quite a lot of time terminating projects and then reallocating funds on the basis of trying to get those efforts updated. That's the way our legislature tries to mandate change unless they happen to give additional money for some special project, which they don't very often do.

Hadwiger: May I ask one question? Is the legislature's committee very directive?

Watts: In Colorado this would be true in terms of the allocation of dollars, but it is not as true in terms of program thrusts. You hear a lot of rhetoric, but it isn't quite what I'd call a decision making kind of input.

Hadwiger: They don't "follow it down," so to speak?

Watts: Oh, they might. They'd be more interested in terms of, "Did you drop off one of your research projects and start twenty new ones?" rather than asking, "Did you really initiate some new energy research programs or some farm research programs, or did your extension program really begin to get a new audience?"

Doerr: I just want to summarize to see if I've understood what you've said in relation to some early questions and statements. Earlier, there were a number of questions addressed which seemed to imply a general view that research has been shaped and formed in its direction by corporate business interests, and some questions were answered in the negative in terms of how much corporate money goes into research. I heard you answering that relationship in quite a different way; namely, that there is a combination of cultural framework and scientific research ethos focused on efficiency and productiveness and profitability and everything else that fed into agribusiness because it became the prime user. This cultural framework and scientific research ethos has to be attacked in addition to challenging the power of the corporate structures.

Hadwiger: Yes, I think so. But, no doubt there are agribusinesses that take an enormous amount of research attention. Let me give you a hypothetical example. Let's say College X has an entomology department and it wants to do a balanced set of research on entomology, but the farmers and the chemical companies keep coming in and asking: "Will this work?" Chemical companies say, "Prove to the farmers that it works. You've got to test it for us." So you end up using all of your resources for that alone. Whose fault is it? Both are at fault. It's a symbiotic thing.

Hessel: There was a phrase in your paper, "strategy of desperation," regarding bankrupt technology. Isn't it important to pursue to what extent we are in that state now, and why? Why have we been going down a particular road for forty years when we've known for some time that it was trouble? A research station especially would know that. Why are we at this stage? It seems to me it has some bearing on this matter of who is controlling the decision making and for what purpose?

Hadwiger: I'd say it was thoughtlessness, an institutional subsystem thoughtlessness. You know that pesticides give you problems, but the economists and maybe some of the rest of the social scientists can take some of the blame because we said, "Well, if you use pesticides you spend three dollars an acre and you get fifteen back." That's a pretty persuasive point. The current situation is similar to one where you have worked your way up into the top of the willows. It was fine while you were going, but you are up there now. Your soil is getting salty, your pesticides don't work, there are all kinds of serious problems, and you're really in a desperate situation, trying somehow to hang on up there. Maybe since that's where your profits come from you ought to do that for the time being. But it seems to me that alternative kinds of agriculture make a lot of sense for our own country as well as for others. Small farm agriculture and related technologies that are labor intensive and require less capital and resource inputs are not only more environmentally responsible, but in some situations are also more efficient, both in terms of output per acre and dollars per acre. Most agricultural scientists who have any linkage with the alternative approach would say, "You're right. You've got to do that." But we're stuck in this tree so to speak, and we don't know how to start another tree alongside.

5 CONTRIBUTIONS OF THE LAND-GRANT SYSTEM: ITS USEFULNESS TO THE UNITED STATES AND ITS POTENTIAL FOR THE LESS DEVELOPED COUNTRIES

J. WENDELL McKINSEY

THE ESSENCE of the contemporary land-grant system is a program of publicly financed research in agricultural production and the distribution of the results of that research directly to farmers, plus a substantially subsidized on-campus program of higher education for students (mostly young people) interested in agriculture. The program also includes research in the processing of agricultural production, and the marketing functions that make it available for consumption in the United States and abroad, and the distribution of those results.

The two questions posed for discussion are: (1) Has this land-grant system made a significant contribution to the welfare of the people of the United States? and (2) Does it have promise of being useful to efforts to increase food availability in the food-short countries of the world? The hypothesis put forward is that the land-grant system has made a significant contribution, and the extension of the essence of that system likely is the best, if not a necessary, avenue for significant increases in food production in the food-short nations.

INDICATORS OF ACHIEVEMENT

The Federal Hatch Act of 1887 gave birth to the federal-state research system identified with the land-grant system, which led to the establishment of agricultural experiment stations in connection with the LGU or college in each of the states. The agricultural extension service was established with the Smith-Lever Act of 1914. The output of this system can best be evaluated by examining the growth of productivity in agriculture, the industry toward which this research is directed.

J. Wendell McKinsey is asst. dean, College of Agriculture, University of Missouri, Columbia, Missouri.

The population of the United States at the time of the passage of the Hatch Act (1887) was about 60 million. Since then, population has grown steadily at a slightly increasing rate (with only one faltering period), multiplying by $3\frac{1}{2}$ in eight decades, approximating 204 million in 1970, and estimated to reach 230 million by 1980. (Note Fig. 5.1 and Table 5.1.) How was increased agricultural production achieved to provide the food necessary for such a growing population? Farm output tripled between 1870 and 1915, remained roughly constant for twenty years to 1935, and has increased even more rapidly since then, except for a brief faltering in the years 1945 to 1950. (Note Fig. 5.2.) The growth in output before 1915 was almost wholly due to the improved acreage brought under cultivation. After 1950 the amount of land employed in agricultural production dwindled, and the farm labor force declined drastically. (Note Figs. 5.3, 5.4, and 5.5.) Agricultural output, in total, has grown dramatically since 1950, but output per acre and output per worker has grown even more dramatically. Figure 5.6 illustrates those two measures for Minnesota agriculture. Whereas, one farm worker supplied enough farm products for fifteen persons in 1950, one farm worker now supplies enough for more than forty-five (see Table 5.2). Figure 5.7 portrays the relatively stable output per unit of (all) input(s) up to 1935, and the rapid increase since that time.

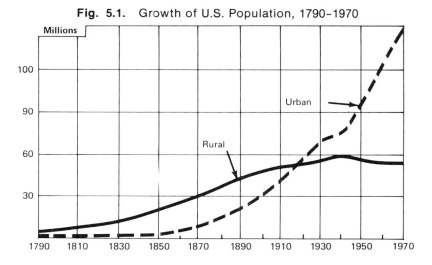

Fig. 5.1. Growth of U.S. Population, 1790–1970

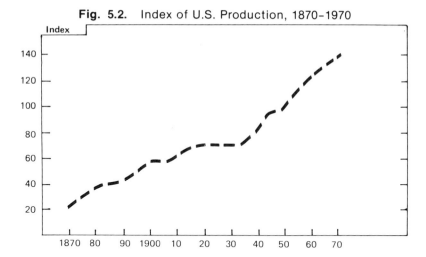

Fig. 5.2.   Index of U.S. Production, 1870–1970

Fig. 5.3.   Index of Land in farms, U.S.

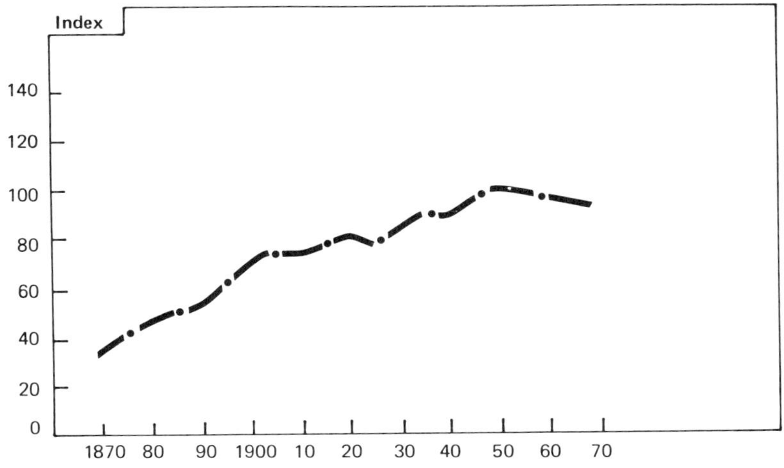

Fig. 5.4. Index of Labor, U.S. Agriculture

The new knowledge generated through the publicly financed research programs has made possible the production of new and improved inputs, and through improved techniques, there has been increased productivity of old inputs. It is true that this period of increased productivity of land and labor has been one of increasing capital input, a significant amount of which was created by research. It is somewhat puzzling that forty years elapsed after the establishment of the public research system before significant results were noticeable in increased agricultural production. Part of the strategy of

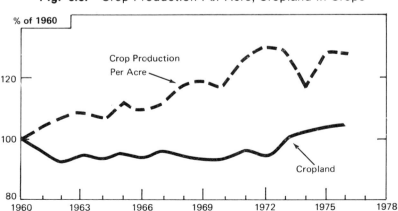

Fig. 5.5. Crop Production Per Acre; Cropland in Crops

Fig. 5.6. Productivity, Minnesota Agriculture

Output per Worker

Output per Acre

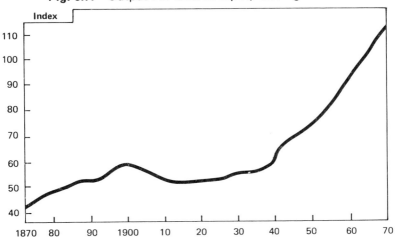

Fig. 5.7. Output Per Unit of Input, U.S. Agriculture

Index

Table 5.1 United States Population, 1880–1970

Year	Total Population, July 1 (millions)
1880	50.3
1890	63.1
1900	76.1
1910	92.4
1920	106.5
1930	123.1
1940	132.1
1950	151.7
1960	179.9
1970	204.0

Table 5.2. Changes in Farm Production and Efficiency; Persons Supplied per Farm Worker

Year	Number
1850	4.2
1900	6.9
1950	15.5
1955	19.5
1960	25.8
1965	37.0
1969	45.3

United States technical assistance is to support developing countries in their efforts to eliminate or significantly shorten the waiting period.

There have been numerous attempts to measure the rate of return on the investment made in agricultural research and extension. Because the calculated rates of return have been so large, investigators continue to reexamine the methods used and try to devise new methods of measurement. A set of data—very conservative in tone—prepared for an international conference at Arlie House in Virginia in 1975, indicated rates of return ranging from 50 percent to 34 percent over the period 1937 to 1972. The evidence is overwhelming. Agricultural research pays handsome rewards.

A UNIQUE SYSTEM

This system of publicly financed research and extension administered through the LGUs is designed for investment in deliberate efforts to extend the frontiers of basic science knowledge;

and from that knowledge, to develop new production technology, or new inputs, or improved inputs; to test new techniques for adaptability; and to communicate the new technology to producer-users.

In a conversation discussing the importance and relevance of such a system in its historical perspective, Herbert F. Lionberger of the Department of Sociology, University of Missouri, observed:

Until well past the turn of the century, invention and discovery was quite exclusively an individual matter. Folk knowledge and an occasional invention by practitioners virtually constituted operating procedures within the then existing specialities. Thus, it was in the professions and farming alike. For them invention was basically within [one's] own social system. In this context, one well-known anthropologist estimated that only one in a thousand inventions survived and became accepted by the public.

When we look at a few examples of how new information and inventions emerged in society and how they were ultimately disseminated to users, we can begin to realize the truly powerful nature of these social inventions. Witness, for example, the different kinds of people who did what, in what order, in what places, over what period of time, to develop such things as a radio or motion pictures. In both cases, it took (1) basic scientists exploring the fundamentals of electronics, light and human perception, nearly always with no desire to do anything more than to extend the frontiers of basic science knowledge; (2) applied scientists who were perhaps more interested in seeing whether they could intervene in the scientific processes than in developing something useful; (3) inventors who just liked to play with their skills (Linton 1936); and (4) developers and distributors mostly interested in making a profit. All of this activity covered at least a century, involved people living on at least two continents, duplicated work, near simultaneous inventions, and subsequent law suits with endless litigation.

In contrast to all of this, imagine an organizational arrangement that puts all of these activities together (basic science, applied science, innovation and dissemination) into a single working arrangement, not as a hobby but as a full-time occupation in a functionally articulated system designed to support the specialized effort at all points on the theory-to-practice continuum plus a capability of preserving almost every new idea or invention. It takes little imagination to recognize the potential power of such a social invention.

Perhaps the first such system emerged in land grant universities over a period of at least 75 years of aborted effort to meet the official charge of teaching agriculture and the mechanic arts to the public. Although the system was mostly oriented to providing specialty agricultural information, it had the organizational capability of developing and supplying virtually any kind of specialty information to any kind of adopter clientele. Professionals here and abroad recognized the potential of these information macrosystem type universities and have attempted to implant them in their own countries to serve both agricultural and other informational speciality needs. But the apparent inclination seems to have been to copy the more tangible organizational and positional features and neglect specifications on how they must work as a functionally articulated whole to produce and deliver a quality informational product. There can be almost no compromise on operational specifications (functions to be performed) but there are organizational alternatives. Also in the diffusion efforts to implant these information macrosystems elsewhere there has been a rather general failure to properly adapt them to the social settings into which they were introduced. Borrowing of such a system without fully understanding how it operates is very much like borrowing an electronic computer without operating instructions.

Because folk knowledge provides an insufficient informational base for virtually every specialized endeavor, development and delivery of a continuous supply of updated information becomes necessary and thus also specialized arrangements for producing and distributing it.

AN ADAPTABLE SYSTEM

Between one-half billion and one billion persons in the world do not receive enough food. Most of them live in the poor countries where populations are growing fastest. The immediate cause of their hunger is the problem of inadequate resources to either buy or produce the food they need. In these poor countries, where most of the hungry are, there isn't enough food, if divided evenly among the population, to provide a minimum adequate diet. Importation of food from more productive countries in sufficient quantities is not feasible. Thus we must look to increased food production in the countries where it is needed, not as the only component of the solution, but as a necessary component.

Food production can be increased through expanding crop area and/or increasing crop production per hectare. Increases in crop area offer significant promise in very few places in the world. Increases in yield are not easy to achieve and sustain, but their possibility and their promise have been demonstrated. The development of improved farming technologies that produce increased yields per unit of land, and perhaps of labor, is needed. An organized effort to produce such "inventions" and disseminate them to the producing farmers is essential to the accomplishment of increased food availability.

Practitioners of agricultural development now well understand that the fruits produced by the land-grant system in this country cannot be duplicated around the world. Nor can the system be transplanted around the world. But the functional requisites of that land-grant system can be the basis or essence of an adapted system essential to produce and disseminate improved technologies, biological innovations, and improved farming systems. Knowledge and experience in the United States land-grant system offers the most productive base from which to develop such locally adapted systems. Research and extension will not solve world food problems, but they are an essential part of the solution.

In fact, a strong research base is essential to all activities needed to increase food supply, reduce poverty, and promote sound government policies. To that end, such a research system has the potential to contribute to the solution of problems beyond that of increased food supply.

Perhaps one of the more promising developments in researching new farm technology for developing countries is the abandonment of the "either-or" syndrome of research here for use there, versus reliance on ill-executed research limited by the poor facilities within developing countries. Instead, joint efforts have been initiated through appropriate linkages between scientists in United States research institutions and scientists in less developed countries' (LDCs) research institutions. Equally important are the increased possibilities for United States scientists to expand the horizons of their own research to international dimensions, and thus expand the knowledge base upon which all agricultural scientists can build.

SUMMARY

There are five main points to be considered when measuring the usefulness of the land-grant system to the United States and its potential for LDCs.

1. The growth of agricultural productivity in the United States is a phenomenon unequaled anyplace else in the world or any other time in history, and is the envy of much of the world's agriculture and many of the governments around the world.

2. Any attempt to explain or understand this phenomenon must emphasize the importance of public investment in deliberate efforts to create or to invent new techniques in agricultural production that lead to increased productivity per unit of land and per person employed. The United States was the first nation to adopt a system of deliberate investment in such efforts.

The system of publicly financed agricultural research and communication which we refer to as extension is a unique social invention in the world. It is based on a policy of service and responsiveness to need. It has been a conscious effort to find new ways to do things and to offer options to farm producers, options which simultaneously increase their productivity as well as enhance their profit in such a system. Profits to the producer are only short-run benefits, but the long-run benefits accrue to the society which made the investment in the form of increased food supply at lower cost.

3. Any solution to the world food problem must include increased production in the food-short nations. Granted, this cannot be the only component, but it is a necessary component.

4. The accomplishment of increased production in the food-short nations necessitates putting in place a system that will do for the agriculture in those LDCs the same two jobs, namely, the creation of new agricultural technology, and the communication of that technology to producer-users. Some of this research can be done here, but a great deal of it must be done in those countries. The United States LGU offers promise as a vehicle to accomplish those purposes.

●

INFORMAL DISCUSSION

McKinsey: The United States was the first country to make major public investments in deliberate efforts to find new ways to do things. I presume that any improvement in the well-being or welfare of an individual or group of individuals comes about by introducing some kind of change in the way things are done. The publicly financed system of research and extension in the United States was a deliberate effort to find ways to change the way things are done in agriculture, to the end of improving the welfare of individuals or groups of individuals.

A major component of the whole land-grant idea has been one of service, or one of responsiveness to need. So far as I know, the scientists working in the colleges of agriculture and the presidents of LGUs are still very much attuned to responding to expressed needs. And those expressed needs come from many sources. They sometimes come from the legislature, they sometimes come from big business, they sometimes come from the pork producers, and they sometimes come in a letter from an individual farmer or consumer. There are various ways in which needs are communicated, and there has been no perfect method developed; there still should be improvement in the way those needs are communicated. But I think if you want to talk about the role of the churches, or any church group of any sort in this effort, this is one of the areas where they can be most effective, and that is as participants in a communication process. In the operating guidelines of the task forces on world hunger of both Presbyterian denominations, there is provision for some effort being spent on sensitizing the church. I think that effort ought to be a good deal larger, because my experience in moving about the Presbyterian church in the state of Missouri has shown me that there are many church people who do not appreciate the relationships between agricultural research and extension and political forces at work in the country, and their possible impact on food supplies in food-short countries. Much work could be done here, and I think this is an awfully important job for the churches to be doing.

Now for a couple of subpoints: (1) It's too bad that we started using this word *extension* around the world, because it has conveyed a particular idea that everybody understood, and understood in the same way. We people in the United States who have been involved in extension work, have been hung-up over questions of organization rather than function. And it's the function that is important. We've begun to use the terminology *communication and technology* rather than the word *extension* because this phrase is more precise. For, in addition to the creation of new ways to do things, it has to be communicated. This is really the problem we're trying to get to. I believe there's a fairly good understanding now of the need to communicate new technology about the world. (2) One of the more promising developments in this whole area of researching new farm technology is the final abandoment of an either/or syndrome of doing research here in this country for use somewhere else, on the one hand, versus the other extreme that all new technological development has to take place in developing, food-short countries. We now have come to the point where we see the most productive arrangement being one in which scientists in the agricultural experiment stations and the research institutions in the United States team up with the scientists and the research institutions in the food-short countries to carry out joint research for the benefit of both parties. We would be less than honest if we denied that the effort were not designed primarily for the benefit of the food-producing system in the developing country. But the instances in which there is mutual benefit are legion, and they are sufficient to warrant support of joint research, even on grounds of national interest.

A corollary opportunity arises now for researchers and agricultural experiment stations in the United States to expand the horizons of their research to international dimensions. Now our scientists can adopt an international horizon and find ways to support that research. This opportunity will expand in the future. It would be completely foolish to expect new technology to be developed in the food-short or developing countries without making use of research that has already been done in the developed countries. It is axiomatic that the more nearly basic the research is, the more nearly transferable it is to any place in the world. And it is also obvious that those solutions that are most demanding of locally adaptive research have to be developed in the area where they are going to be used. There must be some kind of wedding of these two.

Watts: You mentioned the matter of a fifteen dollar return on a three dollar investment as one of the developments that has led us into an escalation of technology. I think that is correct. As you begin to apply technology within a developing country, the political forces—policies that relate to the economics, the distribution, the availability of these products—get into this question in a very, very significant way. Nobody yet has talked about the problem of political dynamics and economic incentives as they relate to the transfer and adoption of technology.

McKinsey: I tried to surface that point in my formal statement. The point I made was that the establishment of research institutions in LDCs designed to deal with agricultural production is essential, but they also need to address the entire gamut of restrictions and problems related to increased food supplies and then develop the right kind of institutions that can address all these problems—agricultural policy, price policy, storage policy, right on down the line.

Pott: I'd like to have you elaborate a little bit on what you describe as provisions for encouraging people who operate in an international context. Part of the problem is that historically, the land-grant colleges have operated out of a state structure, or a state perspective, with the backdrop of a national perspective; but now the challenge is to create international sensitivity and perspective. What did you have in mind?

McKinsey: Title XII of the Act of 1975 authorizes two major activities: joint research and joint agricultural development. The research activity has two components to it: (1) expansion of United States-based research to meet the needs of developing countries or food-short countries; and (2) collaboration between scientists in this country and other countries. Those are the prospects which depend upon the imaginations and creativity of a whole lot of people.

Carlson: On that same point, as a researcher and teacher in this area at a land-grant college, one of the countervailing forces that we have is a reduced budget for training foreign students. Some of this comes in the form of no assistantships for foreign students, or few incentives as researchers to go off into a new area with time to explore new problems of energy use and small-scale farming. So at the federal level, we have, perhaps, some new money for international work, but we have other forces working that give us less chance to work with foreign students. . . .

McKinsey: You remind me of the point I had forgotten a while ago, and I wanted to mention. This ought to interest the church. No state university in the United States has faced up to its constituency in the state in terms of its commitment to international agriculture development because it's afraid to do so. I have made quite a few talks around the state of Missouri to various groups, and I have never yet had an antagonistic audience on this subject; yet we have never admitted to our state legislature our commitment to this, nor has any state legislature I know of (whoever is here from Cornell may possibly contradict me) made a real commitment of its own to its LGU to respond to this international challenge. In the Act of 1975, the Congress declared international agricultural development to be the policy of the United States. But we have not yet gone back to our state legislatures, in whatever way we influence them—through the Kiwanis Club, or the pork producers, or the Presbyterian Church. We've not gone back to them and tried to get some understanding of what we'd like to do.

G. Beran: In our international focus we have faculty persons from here go abroad and work in the developing countries, but we certainly have neglected the role of our students so far in our discussion. Mostly we have talked about how they use up our budgets. Here, about 18 percent of our graduate students come from abroad, and to a very significant extent we are directing their research for their graduate studies toward solving United States problems. We have done pitifully little in working with graduate students from abroad to explore problems that relate specifically to their own countries, and working with them in that area. I had hoped that was going to be your last point.

McKinsey: That's in the next topic that's coming up. There will be three regional, national conferences on that very subject—one at the University of Maryland, one at the University of Illinois, and one at Arizona State University—where land-grant people are getting together to talk about that very problem. I agree with your statement. I don't know that I need to make a response to it; it's a very important element.

Ryan: I have a couple of comments. I think you're accurate in terms of perceptions about current resistance at the state level to funding international research, and I wanted to ask you why you think that is the case. Why is it state legislatures don't like to fund international research? Why don't they see it as a priority?

Hadwiger: They're by definition provincial. I think the answer here is that they don't think they're supposed to do that sort of thing.

Watts: There's a scramble for dollars too. Our legislature put a 7 percent ceiling on the increase in their appropriations this year. Honestly, from a political standpoint, I am not about to ask our legislature for an overseas amount. Part of it is selfishness, and part of it is a misconception. If you fund something (for example, wheat production) it will be competitive, rather than looking at the broader social development of that nation which in the long run will probably give you more market.

McKinsey: Even so, when the Missouri Legislature appropriates money for research at its ag experiment station, they don't tell us what to do with it. That's decided by the president, the dean of research, and a whole group of people that come into the act. The Hatch funds that come from Washington have some kind of provision that specifically prohibits the use of those funds for doing anything other than that which serves the purposes of the United States. But the rest of the funds that come to us do not have any such prohibition, and we use some of those internationally. We don't let the legislature know. I don't know what the legislature would say or do. My point is that as far as I know, every university in the United States is careful to keep that kind of information out of the hands of the legislature. Legislatures do what the public, which elects them, tells them to do, and the Presbyterian Church could have an influence on this if it wanted to.

Knowles: Regarding the training of foreign students, I think it's a place where the church could be heavily involved.

The extension of information in the United States has been a tremendous success story and has been responsible in part for the success of research. In foriegn countries, from my brief experience, skillful interpretation is often lacking. There's lots of good research and good information in the station. They have developed new varieties—good varieties; but neither the variety nor the information moves out, and it's not interpreted, or adapted at the local level.

McKinsey: I appreciate your emphasizing the relationship between research and extension. One is of no account without the other. It's part of one system. No doubt about it, many of us in our first efforts at trying to do something in the food-short countries stressed organization rather than function when we tried to initiate this extension component. There's another whole area in extension work that we didn't get into, and that is the effect of catering to large farms versus small farms. But we don't have time for that today.

Miner: I was just going to comment that one of the problems in sending people to foreign assignments is an assumption among agricultural people that they will lose their technical edge by being gone for more than six months. This gives them very little time to be effective abroad. Many times these assignments are taken by people near retirement, as a reward at the end of their career here.

McKinsey: I'm aware of what you're talking about. I don't know what the church can do about that.

J. Conner: Betty, it's not an assumption, it's a fact.

6 AGRICULTURE AND FOOD POLICY: CURRICULAR CONSIDERATIONS

JERRY D. STOCKDALE

THE HARD-HITTING MESSAGE of anthropologist John Bodley[1] is that just about all development efforts in less developed countries (LDCs) have been very damaging to the tribal or peasant peoples they were designed to help. Bodley documents case after case of development projects gone awry. An extreme interpretation of his position might conclude that since we are never able to anticipate all the negative consequences of our actions we had better not interfere further in the lives of "primitive" and "peasant" peoples. Anything we do is likely to make things worse. Yet Bodley seems to feel that in most cases it is already too late. The developed nations have already interfered much too much and have set negative forces in motion which would continue even if all development efforts were halted. It is a sad picture he presents; out of both evil and noble intentions, the developed nations have torn asunder the fabric of traditional societies and set forces in motion which are not yet fully understood. And he seems to feel that even today projects initiated with the best of intentions are more likely than not to end in a preponderance of negative over positive outcomes and often in disaster.

While Bodley seems to overstate his case, his book, nonetheless, contains evidence which should make each of us uncomfortable, especially those of us who have assumed that increased education, better health, and reduced poverty are directly associated with higher levels of personal satisfaction and well-being. Ironically, studies in our own country also suggest that ever-higher levels of development are not necessarily correlated with higher levels of personal satisfaction.[2]

LIMITED PERSPECTIVES AND BIASES

Bodley's concerns are relevant in several ways to problems of curricular change at LGUs. Most important, Bodley clearly points out the need for much greater attention to a wide range of social,

Jerry D. Stockdale is Head, Department of Sociology, Anthropology, and Social Work, University of Northern Iowa, and was formerly a faculty member at Cornell University.

demographic, environmental, and other impacts of programs which might at first seem to involve only minor technological or social changes. One of my primary concerns with university curricula, especially in agricultural universities, is that it is all too easy for students to graduate with very little understanding of the complexities of social and ecological systems and their interdependencies. Too few graduates understand the importance of analyzing a wide range of potentially very important impacts.

Bodley's argument is also important because it hits many of our biases. Bodley is suggesting that "growth," "progress," "development," and even the ability to grow more food are not always better. This is important to curricular considerations because, just as grade schools tend to be permeated with prodiscipline (law and order) messages, colleges of agriculture have long been permeated by progrowth, protechnology, and other biases.

Listed below are some possible biases or sets of beliefs which may affect the consideration of agricultural and rural development programs and policies. The ideas are presented in pairs. In each case the first item in the pair is one which I would expect to be most prevalent on LGU campuses. In general the items listed second in the pairs are gaining support among Americans. Taken to the extreme, any of the beliefs becomes a bias or presupposition which can be detrimental to effective analysis and policymaking.

Pair 1   Growth is essential (considering alternatives to growth is foolish).
             "No growth" or less growth is imperative now.

Pair 2   Technology will solve all problems.
             Technology creates our problems.

Pair 3   Criticism of agricultural technology increases problems in providing adequate food.
             Scientists in LGUs are "in the pockets" of agribusiness.

Pair 4   Bigger is better (almost always).
             Small is beautiful (almost always).

Pair 5   Increased consumption equals increased personal well-being.
             Increased consumption equals decreased quality of life.

Pair 6   Our culture is superior and thus is an appropriate standard for evaluating other people and cultures (ethnocentrism).
             All aspects of all cultures are equally worth preserving (extreme cultural relativism).

> *Pair 7*   Laissez-faire capitalism is the only acceptable economic system.
>   Capitalism is bankrupt and must be eliminated (by violence if necessary).
> *Pair 8*   Environmental problems would be solved if population growth were limited.
>   The. main source of environmental and resource problems is not population but consumption by the rich nations.
> *Pair 9*   If you can't measure it, it doesn't exist.
>   Everything will be OK if we just "get in touch with our feelings."
> *Pair 10*   We can model anything.
>   The world is so complex we shouldn't even hope to understand it.

In most cases the biases have not been well formed or conscious, and they have been presented in subtle ways. They have nevertheless been pervasive, being shared by large numbers of students, teachers, researchers, and extension workers. This is not surprising since they are so widely diffused through American society.

I well remember the condemnation of Rachel Carson by agriculture college faculty after she published *Silent Spring*. "She is some kind of a nut!" "An odd-ball!" "She cares more about birds than people!" Here is the crux of a core bias. Slightly overstated, the message was: "The most important thing is an ever-increased potential for food production, anything which facilitates that is good, anything which might present obstacles is suspect or pernicious." In our undergraduate, graduate, and early faculty years, it does seem that my peers and I were heavily influenced by this and other biases (see above) which constituted a "hidden curriculum"[3]—by a set of myths, biases, and presuppositions which hindered our ability to analyze political-economic and environmental realities.

Because the ideas just mentioned and those listed above in pairs so strongly influence the assumptions out of which we assess policy alternatives, it is essential that they not remain hidden. It is not possible, nor necessarily desirable, to eliminate all bias, myth, and ideology; but individuals should attempt to understand their biases and, where appropriate, attempt to minimize their impact. Where particular biases are ubiquitous in educational institutions, it is important that this be known. "Hidden curricula" should be avoided by reducing biases, presenting alternative perspectives, or, at least, bringing the biases into the open.

The issue of biases has been emphasized here because (with

Bodley) I feel that all too often programs concerned with increasing food production have involved activities which have been detrimental to the dignity and well-being of people they were designed to assist. More bluntly, the "hidden curriculum" to which I was exposed contained a number of biases that are inappropriate to policymaking in agricultural and rural development.

My major philosophic difference from Bodley is that I am more optimistic in my belief that it is possible to be responsive to problems and to do so in a responsible way. That so many mistakes have been made in the past does not mean that the future is hopeless. But some special people, skills, and perspectives are needed, and the LGUs have an important part to play in developing them.

DESIRED CHARACTERISTICS OF GRADUATES

Based on the preceding assumptions, some characteristics can be listed which would seem to be related to effective and responsible involvement in agricultural and rural development programs. These include: specific knowledge and skills, breadth of perspective, willingness to be critical, flexibility, openness, self-awareness, awareness of political-economic realities, and willingness to get one's hands dirty.

First and foremost the person must have knowledge and skills. It is essential that graduates have expertise relevant to the particular problems they will be working with whether they involve plant breeding, livestock diseases, nutrition, engineering, or whatever. The issue of relevance is important here, however. Increasingly it is recognized that some types of information and skills which are useful for persons in United States commercial agriculture have little applicability to LDC situations. Capital-intensive Iowa agriculture, for example, is very different from the situation in Tanzania, where approximately 90 percent of the population is involved in agriculture, most shambas (farms) have fewer than $2\frac{1}{2}$ acres, the most common and in many cases the only tool is the hoe, nearly half the population is under fifteen years of age, adult literacy is low, and where labor is surplus and capital is very scarce. Basic physical, biological, and social principles may be the same but their application will often be very different. Thus the concern for "appropriate technology" is one to which LGUs must give increasing attention if they are to be of optimum value in preparing persons to work effectively in LDC agriculture and rural development situations. The long-standing concern in LGUs for developing technical competence and expertise must be maintained. Increasing attention, however, should be given to designing such teaching to maximize its usefulness to students from LDCs and others interested in working in LDC situations.

While specific kinds of knowledge and expertise are extremely important, they are far from adequate. It is important that graduates attain breadth of perspective and knowledge in a wide range of areas. Awareness of complexities and coherence in ecological and social systems is increasingly important for persons involved in development activities.

Closely related to breadth of perspective is the need for a critical (questioning) perspective in assessing information and alternatives. Policymakers, especially, should be sensitive to the range of possible short- and long-term costs and benefits of alternative technologies, programs, and policies.

While the graduate should be critical, he/she should also be flexible—able to assess ideas and programs on the basis of information rather than biases and unexamined predispositions.

It is also essential that graduates be open to cultural differences and not overly ethnocentric. This is especially important in working in LDCs where the underlying values, beliefs, and rationales for action may not be immediately apparent. Lack of such openness can lead not only to the "ugly American" phenomenon but also to failure to predict accurately human behavior in development activities. When ethnocentrism leads to a lack of respect for local people it is also likely to result in failure to consider vital information and perspectives.

It is important that graduates attain high levels of self-awareness. This does not mean extreme "turning inward"; but rather it implies understanding and acceptance of self which allows and facilitates effective, responsible, and humanistic involvement in vital issues. As much as possible graduates should be aware of the sources of their own actions, including their beliefs, values, and world views. It is essential that they learn not to be afraid of the subjective, that they "get in touch with their feelings," that they temper logic and rationality with empathy and sensitivity. People are needed who are "hardheaded" yet sensitive, realistic yet with ideals and aspirations. More generally, the students should develop understanding of human behavior which goes beyond common sense.

Since many LDCs are "political hotspots," it is also important that graduates have at least a minimal understanding of political-economic realities, including the ideological underpinnings of capitalism and communism; international patterns of resource allocation and inequality, and of neocolonialism and economic exploitation. It is essential that anyone working in development programs in LDCs clearly understand that the long-term net flow of resources on a worldwide scale has been and continues to be from the poor nations to the rich.

A final desirable characteristic for any graduate who will be involved in development efforts is the willingness to get one's hands dirty. A frequent complaint of leaders in LDCs is that once young people from the villages get some education they are no longer willing to work with their hands and in some cases are not even willing to return to rural areas. This is less a problem in the United States, especially among graduates of LGUs, but it is still a matter of concern. Many important agricultural development opportunities are to be found in the villages developing appropriate technologies. It may not be academically appropriate for LGUs to teach such practical self-reliance skills as how to tear down, fabricate parts for, and rebuild a Land Rover; or such tricks as cutting up a bicycle tube for a temporary water hose for a Peugot. Such skills are, however, essential in some LDC situations. University faculty, especially those in LDC situations, should strive to resist the appearance in students of elitist attitudes, awe of complex technology, and aversion to physical work.

While it is not realistic for university faculties to expect to instill all such knowledge, characteristics, and patterns of thought in all or even most graduates, there are some factors which can be manipulated to maximize the extent to which the goals are attained. Probably the most important influences are curriculum content and faculty characteristics.

CURRICULUM

It is possible to move directly from the preceding to some prescriptions for curricular change. First, if the goals are to be accomplished, it is essential that narrow, technical specializations be avoided and that students, regardless of their majors, be exposed to a broad set of "general education" or "distributive" courses. The preceding considerations suggest what some of these nonmajor courses should be. Table 6.1 contains a listing of such courses. It is important to remember that much important learning in university communities takes place in nonacademic settings. Campus ministries, for example, have an important opportunity to help in the development of concerned, sensitive, and responsible graduates and faculty.

It would not be unrealistic to expect students on a quarter system to complete each of the courses listed in Table 6.1 nor for students in a semester system to complete all the courses in the middle column. It is expected, however, that many students and some faculty in colleges of agriculture would resist a move to insert this many social science and humanities courses, arguing that the students need the time for chemistry, biology, and agriculture courses. Such an argument is in direct opposition to a main theme of this paper which is that overspecialization has been a major problem in the past and is a possible serious pitfall for the future. It is essential that students be exposed to the kind of courses listed in Table 6.1 in order that they move toward becoming the critical, flexible, open, self-aware, broadly knowledgeable persons who will be needed in an increasingly problematic future.

Table 6.1. Courses to be Completed by All Students in B.S. or B.A. Degree Programs

Content Area	Essential Courses	Strongly Recommended Courses
Natural sciences	Intro. Biology Ecology Intro. Chemistry Intro. Physics	
Social sciences	Intro. Sociology Social & Cultural Anthropology People & Cultures of the World Intro. Psychology Social Psychology Micro Economics Macro Economics Social Ecology[a]	Social Problems American Government Comparative Political Systems International Economics Population & Demography World Poverty & Dependency[b]
Humanities	Intro. Literature Intro. Philosophy	Unites States History European History Non-Western History, e.g., China, India
Other	Writing Fundamentals (demonstrate competence) Intro. Statistics	Speech Mathematics Logic

[a] The social ecology course should be taught from an interdisciplinary, social science perspective and should contain content on: problems of resource depletion and environmental degradation; relationships among social organization, culture, technology, environment, population, and quality of life variables; forces influencing resource allocation and consumption decisions; and selected resource, environmental, social, and personal impacts of technology and policy alternatives.

[b] The world poverty and dependency course should be taught from an interdisciplinary, social science perspective. Poverty should be analyzed as an aspect of national and international systems. Students should be encouraged to examine poverty as a problem of both development and oppression. The concepts of internal colonialism and/or dependency should be used to illustrate structural similarities between some domestic poverty and many LDC situations. The net flow of resources from the poor to the rich nations and from rural to urban places should be emphasized.

Since many students in colleges of agriculture will become involved, at one time or another, in international agricultural development programs, it is also important that they gain basic knowledge in the agricultural sciences and that a variety of courses with international emphasis be available to them. Students who plan to work in LDC agricultural situations, regardless of their specialities, should understand the basics of crops, soils, animal science, agricultural engineering, agricultural economics, and rural sociology. The World Poverty and Dependency course (described at the bottom of Table 6.1) should be required of all such students. While it is expected that some universities will continue to emphasize international programs more than others do, a variety of international courses should be available to students at all LGUs.

Although graduate studies are usually considered to be a time for specialization in highly technical areas, some consideration of breadth of perspective is needed here, also, especially for students who are graduates of overly specialized undergraduate programs and who plan to be involved in development projects in LDCs. For such students, serious consideration should be given to requiring social science and international content in their graduate programs. Courses in social and cultural anthropology, ecology, and social-ecology would be especially important, as would courses concerned with the realities of development and of resource allocation and consumption on a worldwide scale.

Simply adding courses is not sufficient. Faculty advisors have an extremely important part to play in encouraging both undergraduate and graduate students interested in international work to take the kinds of courses which will best prepare them.

MORE MAVERICKS NEEDED

The transmission of technical information and skills is and should continue to be the primary emphasis in most courses in LGUs. Professional competence should be the primary consideration in all hiring and retention decisions. Fortunately these ideas are consistent with changes which are likely to make LGUs more responsive and responsible in the future. I am referring to what I perceive as a breakdown in the old patterns of bias and myth. The "hidden curriculum" is no longer hidden. It has been attacked from without and at many levels from within. The old biases still exist, but alternative perspectives seem to be gaining visibility and respectability. It is my impression that the LGUs are increasingly being staffed by faculty who are professionally competent but who are to some extent "mavericks." They are not mavericks in ways which pose major threats to their universities but in their questioning of the way things are and of accepted notions about how they should be. They ask penetrating and sometimes embarrassing questions. This is not only good; it is essential. Given the importance of LGUs to agricultural and rural development, it is essential that they strive to expose students to diverse perspectives and approaches.

By a maverick I mean a person who is willing to do research which he/she knows is likely to result in unpopular conclusions, with the selection of the problem being on the basis of its importance rather than the political acceptability of the likely conclusions. And when the research is done, the findings are presented honestly and forcefully regardless of whether Eli Lilly, A. J. Reynolds Tobacco, Iowa Beef Producers, or selected alumni are likely to disapprove of them. In the classroom the maverick is willing to raise issues about likely employment, resource, and environmental impacts of technological innovations and to challenge students to examine their own assumptions and perspectives. The maverick is the kind of person who will confront students with unpleasant but vitally important realities, such as the extent and negative effects of inequality both at home and internationally and the continuing exploitation of the LDCs by the "developed" countries. The maverick presents a variety of perspectives and analyses but refuses to distort the picture in favor of the conventional wisdom or the popular position. The maverick is willing to confront the biases listed earlier in the chapter. The maverick is "hardheaded," rational, and realistic about how things are but at the same time sensitive to both problems and possibilities.

Hiring is one way to bring the desired characteristics to LGUs. Faculty development is another. While this will not necessarily be easy, it is essential that strong efforts be made to help sensitize faculty members to their own biases, lack of breadth, and provincialism where these hinder effective performance. It seems likely that many faculty members would be pleased to examine their own assumptions and presuppositions, to broaden their areas of knowledge, and to gain international experience if they perceived realistic opportunities and rewards for doing so. Such efforts are already underway at some LGUs.[4] If these and other such efforts are to be successful, it is essential that they receive support from within and outside the universities. Campus ministries could play an important part in encouraging and supporting examination of assumptions by faculty and increased self-awareness.

While mavericks will not always be as competent, unselfish, and serene as portrayed above and while we should not look for perfection in our mavericks, there are further qualities which would greatly increase their effectiveness. They should be well grounded in theory and research, be productive, be able to assimilate information and formulate appropriate responses quickly, be effective in both written and verbal communication, and be dynamic teachers. I know some people who have these characteristics. Some of them are faculty members at LGUs. There should be more.   ●

INFORMAL DISCUSSION

Stockdale: As a postscript, I do want to make one general comment; namely, I wonder if any of you had the same nostalgic feeling as I did driving here today. I can remember when snow in Iowa used to be white. I don't know if you saw it, but I saw an awful lot of snow that looked like it had at least an eighth of an inch of soil covering wide areas. Is that a sign of progress or of disaster?

Gibson: In discussing biases isn't it necessary to get beyond just seeming to imply that if we just expose the fact that we have biases, we will all be rational enough to want to get beyond our biases? The thing that is not dealt with is the extent to which there are vested interests operative in preserving the biases. It seems to me that your topic is really values, but it stresses the social science view that people ought to have a general education, and then you admit that such education in itself isn't going to do the job. Why isn't it going to do the job? Because the crux of the matter is what these people really care about. Are they really getting this education, doing this research, or teaching because they want poor people to eat, or because they want professional advancement themselves?

Stockdale: Well, one of the assumptions I've made is that LGU faculty members in the past have had a set of biases they weren't even aware of themselves, and if you can call the perspectives to the attention of the people who have the perspectives, and if they don't like what they see when they perceive the values behind their actions, you may bring about some change just by helping them realize what's going on. The church has a real role to play in that kind of situation, by helping to sensitize people to some of the crucial issues in the world today and to some of the ways of looking at world situations which are actually detrimental to change or improvement in those situations. So, I think your point is a good one. Those biases/values aren't just free floating out there. There are reasons why they exist, but the times are changing and what is an appropriate set of ideas, an appropriate way of looking at the world at sometime in the past, may not be appropriate today.

To take a related point—I think some of the environmental problems may actually be solved by the functioning of the economic marketplace, though I don't like to say that's ever going to be a solution. For example, as the price of energy goes up, it may be more effective in cutting back our waste of energy than any exhortations any of us can give. Times change, and as old ways of looking at the world become less appropriate and less useful, then maybe those ways of looking at the world will change. In fact, that's what I see happening.

Rogers: You're the first one so far, except perhaps Bill Gibson, who's dared to tiptoe up to the ideological question. You speak of biases, while I agree with Bill you're talking about the evidence of something a lot deeper and more powerful than biases, I don't think it's just interest. It's something very deep in our history, and I think the universities are in danger of fostering antiintellectualism by not dealing more frankly with the ideological question. I'm talking about alternative systems and ideologies that compete with our interests in the Third World. I think we're not very fair about how they operate, or how they produce, and why people are committed to those alternatives. I'm glad you tiptoed up to it, and I wish you'd take hold of it a little more firmly.

Stockdale: Maybe that's a result of my education in the land-grant system.

Hessel: I was going to make some suggestions for Table 6.1. I think it's a little short in the humanities area, specifically in comparative religions. It seems to me if we're serious about values and ideology, we also should explore the connection between ideology and theology. It is possible to study religion without running into all the problems of church and state, especially if you get into comparative studies of religion. The other thing I was looking for in Table 6.1 is the connection between what I'd call a domestic colonialism and the problems of LDCs which I think would be beautifully illustrated in any state that is heavily agricultural. Rural America is essentially a domestic colony, just as internationally we are the metropole and the other countries are the hinterlands. The same thing happens in this country; there could be more study of the parallels in underdevelopment, or de-development, or overdevelopment in this society and overseas. Some ag school students come out of communities that are colonial, with institutional structures that suffer the fate of a colonial society. All the services are decaying. You can't even go to a store anymore in some of these towns because all the retail chains are moving away. The same holds true for educational opportunities or job opportunities. I think that a lot more could be done terms of comparative perspectives on colonialism.

Stockdale: I see that as one of many, many issues that I would like to help make students conscious of, and you can't have a course on every issue. The question is: How do you put together courses? That's a real problem with the idea of having courses, and that's why I emphasize the role of the faculty. I think that social problems courses in sociology departments should deal with the implications of colonialism. Some do and some don't. If students happen to hit a course where they do get into this issue, that's taken care of, but if they happen to get one where they don't it's not. It's difficult to figure out how to put all of these courses in the curriculum. I have my biases too; I'd like to insist that every student have a course in social stratification and a course in political sociology, but I happen to teach both of those courses.

Knowles: I would like to interject my bias. The spectrum of courses that you would recommend for a person who is going out in an advisory capacity to a developing country is very short on professional courses. Yet you emphasized that professional competency had top priority.

Stockdale: Well, these are courses to be taken in addition to their major or minor. These are courses every undergraduate student should take regardless of major or minor.

Knowles: But suppose your major is animal husbandry or animal science. You should have a good course in the principles of crop production. I don't mean "how-to" courses, but 80 percent of the food produced in a poor country comes from field crops and to some extent horticultural crops. I feel if you're going to send anybody abroad, one of the compulsory courses should be a good one in principles of field crop production. A course in water management in which you're taught irrigation is essential because in many countries you're going to help, you're going to get involved in water management sooner or later. Another necessary course is entomology because when you get out there, there are going to be no entomologists within a thousand miles who can help you identify things. And then comes plant pathology. I'm just listing some of the basic courses we require in the curriculum in plant science at the University of California.

Stockdale: I agree with the point you're making. In an earlier draft I had this list of courses, and then a list that was for ag students in addition to this. Everyone should have a course in soils, a course in crops, a course in animal husbandry, and a course in ag engineering. I thought perhaps the students' major would require them to get some of those courses, and I also thought if I listed too many courses here, it would seem unrealistic.

McKenzie: There's an awful lot that goes into the making of a man or a woman, and one of those things is the courses that they took in the university. The best cooks I know never had a course in cooking. The most imaginative, creative people I've seen overseas never took your list of courses. Somehow or other somebody inspired them, got their curiosity fired up, and they keep on learning and learning and learning.

Stockdale: I agree in general, but I do think it's unfortunate that the other people and I who graduated from Iowa State with undergraduate degrees in agriculture didn't have a broader knowledge of the humanities and social sciences.

McKenzie: I think we made a great big mistake in your and my time. I had five courses that I could choose and all of the rest were prescribed. Right now at the University of Missouri some students can choose their curriculum with the advice of a faculty committee.

Stockdale: Some of the things I'm suggesting already are being considered by people in LGUs, and the key points made here regarding the need for breadth and humanities for land-grant college students will receive more attention in curriculum reform.

7 TEACHING WORLD FOOD ISSUES IN THE UNIVERSITIES

GEORGE W. BERAN

THE TEACHING of world food issues to university students in the classroom and research laboratory is a unique opportunity and responsibility. The primary target student populations are the United States students preparing for various forms of participation in feeding the people of the world, and foreign students from food-needy nations who are in American universities preparing for careers in their own lands. The problems of feeding the world's population, along with the problems of controlling the increase in that population, rank among the top international issues. Students whose careers will involve any areas of feeding the people of food-deficit nations can be helped by courses focusing on world food issues.

This report details preliminary findings in a survey of world food issues courses offered in the forty-seven LGUs in the United States. At this time, information has been received from twenty-two of these universities. All twenty-two universities offer courses with specific international focuses on food issues; the numbers vary from 1 to 44 with a median of eight courses. All offer one or more such courses with a multidisciplinary perspective and are designed for students in a number of academic majors or in off-campus extension classes, and 91 percent of the universities also offer one or more courses in specific aspects of world food issues. These latter courses, offered by specific university departments primarily for their major students, make up 71 percent of the world food issues courses. Only 18 percent of the universities offer undergraduate specialties in food-related areas within an international studies co-major, and only 9 percent currently offer such a graduate major.

The courses offered by the responding universities center around three major broad objectives: (1) to expand the students' knowledge and capability in international aspects of their major fields; (2) to develop an understanding of international needs and problems in feeding the people of the world; and (3) to develop an awareness of the

George W. Beran is professor, College of Veterinary Medicine, Iowa State University, Ames.

roles of other professionals in the total effort and of the levels of interaction needed.

Courses offered in LGUs which deal with subject areas in world food issues as portions of courses or as entire courses are summarized in Table 7.1. Economics departments are most frequently involved in food issues courses, with 90 percent of the universities offering courses focusing on economics of international development, and 67 percent offering one to ten entire courses in this area. Plant Science departments are the second most frequently involved, with 86 percent offering courses focusing on world crop production and 57 percent offering one to six entire courses in this area. This is in marked contrast to courses focusing on world animal production which are offered by only 62 percent of the universities and in world fisheries and seafoods which are offered by only 28 percent of the universities. Also ranking high in offerings are courses focusing on world population issues (86 percent), national and international food policies (76 percent), technology of food production (76 percent) and handling and processing (71 percent), and in nutrition and health (71 percent). Only a few universities offer courses specifically focusing on world environmental issues (38 percent), on international education, extension, and communications (33 percent), on world climatology (28 percent), and on international diseases and pests of plants and animals (19 percent).

Table 7.1. Courses in World Food Issues in Land-Grant Universities

Subject Areas in World Food Issues	% of Universities Teaching Subject	
	Included	Entire Course(s)
Economics of International Development	90	67
World Crop Production	86	57
World Population Issues	86	24
National and International Food Policies	76	33
Food Production Technology	76	10
Nutrition and Health in Developing Countries	71	38
Food Technology in Developing Countries	71	10
International Trade in Food	67	24
World Soils	62	29
World Animal Production	62	19
World Energy and Natural Resource Utilization	57	19
Sociology and International Development	52	24
World Environmental Issues	38	24
International Education, Extension, Communications	33	21
World Climatology	28	10
World Fisheries and Seafoods	28	5
International Diseases and Pests of Plants and Animals	19	5

Iowa State University, with an enrollment of 22,800 for 1977–1978 school year, has drawn 6.4 percent of its students from abroad. Among these students, 91 percent are from developing countries and 26 percent are in food-related curricula. Fourteen academic courses are currently offered with specific focuses on world food issues. Overall class enrollments have varied from six to forty students. Foreign students have comprised 16.7 percent of undergraduate and 33.3 percent of graduate student enrollments in these courses, which brings foreign student enrollment below a desired level. Table 7.2 shows offerings and enrollment data for eight courses for students in a variety of major fields. Five academic departments offer the seven courses designed principally for undergraduate and one course for graduate students. The two broadest based courses, "Introduction to World Food Problems" and "World Food Issues" are newly organized for Spring, 1978. "Introduction to World Food Problems" and "Environment and Society" are offered both to off-campus extension and to on-campus students. Table 7.3 shows offerings and enrollment data for six courses offered for majors in specific departments. Four departments offer three principally undergraduate and three principally graduate courses for their students.   ●

INFORMAL DISCUSSION

G. Beran: The courses that are offered in the LGUs which deal in these subject matters are summarized in the first table: the basic courses and the number of universities that include these at least as part of a course and then, secondly, who offer an entire subject in this area—one or more.

ECONOMICS OF INTERNATIONAL DEVELOPMENT. The economic departments predominate—90 percent offering material in economics of international development, economics of foreign trade, and economics of export products.

WORLD CROP PRODUCTION. Most of the universities offer at least parts of courses.

POPULATION ISSUES. Few universities offer a specific course in population. Most of them include it in some other courses such as sociology. Twenty-four percent have a specific course.

NATIONAL AND INTERNATIONAL FOOD POLICIES AND POLITICS. These are offered to a great extent under political science departments. Seventy-six percent of the universities have such material included.

FOOD PRODUCTION TECHNOLOGY. Seventy-five percent of the universities explore it on an international basis, most of them as part of overall courses in world food issues.

Table 7.2 Courses in World Food Issues, Iowa State University, with Interdisciplinary Emphases

I. Courses with Interdisciplinary Emphases

Course Title	Offering Department	Times Offered	Class Size Range		Student Level	
			All Students	Foreign	Undergrad.	Grad.
Principally for Undergraduate Students						
Climates of the Continents	Agronomy	>3	25-30	1-2	20-25	5
Intermediate Technology	Agric. Mechanization	1	6	...	6	0
Introduction to World Food Problems	University Studies	New	...	...	...	Not open
Seminar on World Food Problems	Food Technology	>3	8-10	2	7-10	0-1
Population and Food	University Studies	4	30-35	3-4	30-35	Not Open
Environment and Society	University Studies	9	10-30	0	0	10-30
Adoption and Diffusion	Sociol. & Anthropol.	>3	35-40	2-3	25-30	10
Principally for Graduate Students						
World Food Issues	Universtiy Studies	New	...	...	...	...

Table 7.3. Courses in World Food Issues, Iowa State University, Designed for Student Majors by Departments

II. Courses Designed for Student Majors in Offering Departments

Course Title	Offering Department	Times Offered	Class Size Range		Student Level	
			All Students	Foreign	Undergrad.	Grad.
Principally for Undergraduate Students						
World Soil Resources	Agronomy	7	15-20	1-2	10-15	5
World Crops	Agronomy	>20	20-25	4-5	16-20	4
World Food Politics	Political Science	4	15-20	0-1	12-16	3-4
Principally for Graduate Students						
Ecology of World Crops	Agronomy	16	15-24	8-12	0-1	14-24
Sociology of Adoption and Diffusion	Sociol. & Anthropol.	3	10-12	5-6	Not Open	10-12
Agriculture in the World Economy	Economics	8	10-15	5-7	0-1	9-15

NUTRITION AND HEALTH. This looms quite large. Most of the universities have at least one course on nutrition/health in developing countries.

INTERNATIONAL TRADE IN FOOD. A large number of universities cover this.

WORLD SOILS. This course is often included along with world crop production. A number of universities offer courses in soils of the world.

Less frequent courses are world animal production, world energy and natural resource utilization, sociology of international development, world environmental issues, education/extension and communications, world climatology, world fisheries and sea foods, plant and animal diseases and pests. We have an imbalance in terms of courses on world food issues being offered to students in LGUs.

In the undergraduate, interdisciplinary courses we offer here [Iowa State], shown in Table 7.2, none of the class size ranges has been huge. Foreign students have been relatively conspicious by their absence, and the few who took a course have been mainly undergraduates.

The interdisciplinary graduate course on world food issues attracts American students who have an interest in working abroad. Foreign students have gone into the courses that are offered within their own disciplines. If the courses relate to world issues, they have taken them, but they have not come into these interdisciplinary courses in any numbers at all. I really wish we could focus on this; the international student who has taken a very tightly organized course in agronomy comes here for graduate study and is channeled into agronomy. The international student does not move over into other interdisciplinary courses. We need to be working on this. Maybe it's important in courses on agronomy, world crops, and similar topics to design them to cover a broader scope because we are not going to get foreign students to take the interdisciplinary courses.

Courses principally for graduate students (for those in specific majors)—ecology of world crops, sociology of adoption and diffusion, agriculture and the world economy—have a fair representation of foreign students compared to the American students. At Iowa State University foreign students have made up some 33 percent of our graduate student enrollment in graduate food issues courses, but they have been in the courses offered by specific departments rather than in the interdisciplinary ones. The two broadest based courses are introduction to world food problems and world food issues which are newly organized this quarter. They have not attracted foreign students.

B. Baker: Are any of your staff foreign?

G. Beran: Yes, we have quite a sizeable population from other countries.

B. Baker: I mean teaching these courses.

G. Beran: Yes, we do have a number of guest lecturers who are international persons, as well as a number of teachers who are teaching entire courses. We have also a variety of other courses that relate to governments in Asia, governments in Africa, and other areas in the Third World.

Stockdale: I notice that a number of the courses are offered in the University Studies program. Could you briefly say what that program is?

G. Beran: The University Studies program is an interdisciplinary program in which students at the undergraduate level can select courses from all over the university. There is a very wide range of courses, with few specific requirements. They can get a degree then in University Studies. At the graduate level they can get a minor within this area.

Stockdale: Is it a department with its own faculty? Or does it draw faculty?

G. Beran: It's an interdisciplinary program, and it's directly under the office of the academic vice-president.

Stockdale: Does that mean that people from different disciplines are together in a department, or that there is no real faculty—just drawing on people as needed?

G. Beran: That's right. There is no real department. There is an advisory committee composed of people from all over the university. Specific courses draw on people from almost anywhere.

Shoemaker: North Carolina State in Raleigh has a similar department.

B. Baker: We have a program at Oregon State called Honors. That's how campus ministers get their foot in the door. They teach courses in the Honors program.

Hessel: Do any of these reports indicate efforts to learn in living situations, or dormitory situations, as distinct from the formal classroom? For example, Whitworth College started a Nutrition 1985 Program, involving a whole dorm. They contracted with a food service which initially costs more than the regular service. The students could actually pay for at least a semester-long new eating experience. You build a lot of informal, and to some degree structured, presentations around that whole eating experience. It's all contracted; everyone knows what they're getting into. There's nothing complicated about the arrangements. All you do is make sure enough people sign up. That model has been written up in our Hunger Notebook. They've done it very successfully at Whitworth. They can probably influence the food services generally with some ideas. Has anything like that showed up? Who's staying with whom? Maybe a group of students who want to concentrate in this field are spending a lot of time together outside of class.

G. Beran: Nothing of that kind showed up. A lot of the universities have programs of travel abroad that relate to food—not just to social structure—that do specifically relate to world food and students are given credit for living abroad in certain planned arrangements. But nothing of the kind of program you describe—a simulation game of doing it right here. Tremendous idea. I wonder if anybody in any LGU has tried it.

Shoemaker: North Carolina is, next semester, in connection with the University Studies program on Food and Population Issues.

Miner: Our university offers the alternate feeding line.

G. Beran: That would be for Asian food or Latin American food?

Miner: It's for vegetarians. You wouldn't find that out by writing the agricultural department. You have to write to home economics.

Stockdale: Did you get any feedback in terms of whether there's a positive reinforcement by the university to encourage more students to take these courses. If so, by what means were students enabled to take these courses?

G. Beran: The University of Minnesota responded rather positively in that way. They commissioned a group of their faculty to do a study on this very thing and to put out a little booklet which they have distributed through the departments and have designated specific faculty persons within each department, who are interested in international studies, to serve as advisers for students who want this emphasis. Cornell rather similarly; Michigan State also has a booklet in this area that students can get. We don't.

Stockdale: I was very interested to see the Adoption and Diffusion course listed, because before I shortened my remarks, I digressed to point out that my own field of sociology really hasn't done too well, and has not faced up to these issues. Most LGUs used to have a course in Adoption and Diffusion where we taught how to get people to use new and improved technology. I'm not criticizing that course; I think it's a good course. But we almost never have had courses where we looked at the implications of the technology being used. I was hoping that by now the land-grant colleges had courses where they looked at the implications. I'm somewhat disappointed that my own alma mater and the department I graduated from still have the Adoption and Diffusion course, which they should have, but don't pursue the implications.

J. Beran: I would like to comment on the fact that the most often offered course is in international economics. What does that say about

LGUs? Is economics the most important factor? The other subjects are not stressed. What effect is this having?

Stockdale: I took that course many years ago. What I remember about it was that we studied the European Economic Community, the Common Market. That was the emphasis of the course. I don't remember that it had anything to do with Third World countries.

Pott: Are there any developments, comparable to the Junior Year Abroad which private liberal arts institutions have sponsored for so long, that would give students the experience of adapting technology in the environment of an underdeveloped country?

G. Beran: It tends to be a tour. That's a seeing thing, not a doing thing.

Miner: We have one. You can select what year you want to go, and we're offering credit for travel and study in Japan, France, or Germany under the supervision of a resident university person, and then they usually take university courses. There are really no developing countries in this program.

J. Beran: Was there any comment in the questionnaires as to why there were so few foreign students? Is part of the problem the fact that the major advisers of graduate students, or major professors, do not see the signficance of these courses? Is it the advising that is at fault?

G. Beran: Nobody philosophized on this. Is it in part the graduate student, as well, hesitating to go into a course he might get a "C" in, when by staying within his own discipline he can get a "B"?

J. Beran: It would be interesting to have a follow-up study on the research topics of foreign graduate students and see how much is applied research, applicable to where they came from. Along with that, the study should correlate the rate of return (to home country) of graduate students, though this is hard to identify. Does anyone know of a survey of dissertations of graduate students from abroad?

B. Baker: We find that the students are often sent by very specific people—officials of corporations and governments—with explicit instructions on what they should be able to do when they return home. This doesn't leave very much for any but required courses in the limited time they have here. They arrive very task oriented; do it and go home. Occasionally they get into something else. We also found them unaware of problems in their homeland.

G. Beran: I absolutely agree; their lack of awareness is typical because they come from the capital city and have been far from the agricultural situation that comprises 70 percent of their own land.

Shoemaker: The vaues are often so different. We were often very surprised to find that extreme poverty or death from starvation is not considered a problem in some areas. It's a fact of life.

G. Beran: We have a rather poor track record here of getting students and preparing students to go back to their own countries. Many who come from countries where knowledge of English is limited, develop a technical knowledge of English but do not develop a social knowledge of English, seem to go back to their country more often. But those who come here from countries where they speak English as a very prominent second language, and who speak it both socially and technically, tend not to go back. A great number of those that do go back are misfits within their own country, and they bounce back to this country, or Canada, like a cork out of water again. A very significant part of our graduate emphasis is geared to American problems and not to problems of these countries. We do not have a program here to which a graduate student can come, do his course work, go back to his own country, do his thesis, and be examined in some manner through the university within his own country and receive his degree.

Hessel: I was wondering about the domestic connection. In most of the major denominations we say world hunger, world food issues; we deliberately want to include, and we want everyone to define the subject as including, domestic hunger in the United States. Was there any lead in your questionnaire which would cause them to make the connection? That kind of dimension really ought to be built into world food issues teaching. I was wondering what you would like to see done along that line.

G. Beran: The only thing that came out fairly frequently was that our universities do, within their courses in nutrition and public health, discuss malnutriton and food problems in the United States. Most of those topics are treated in home economics or in some health-related area, but to do that in a world food issues course—no. It doesn't show up at any point.

B. Baker: I noticed your statistics for twenty-two thousand students. Even thirty people in a class isn't very many Americans. I would assume that if we get ten or twelve in a class on interdependent world issues, most of us would find that exciting. I don't know if there are any thoughts on these low enrollments, but I would like to talk about it a little bit.

G. Beran: Our upper level courses don't run very large.

Hadwiger: Are advisers really informed about these things? Are advisers generally oriented to world food problems?

B. Baker: Or even the university studies sort of course?

G. Beran: It takes tremendous initiative on the part of the student to find them, doesn't it?

Shoemaker: We find that buying an ad in the student paper helps to advertise those specific courses.

G. Beran: We have one teacher here in the university who advertises in the paper and it has become such a stigma that the other two thousand or so of us just don't do it.

Killmer: Was there any indication of the racial background of the people taking these courses? I'm thinking of American students.

G. Beran: No, no such indication. I don't think that I could get that kind of information here for our own students.

Killmer: It strikes me as a very important question for a number of reasons, including whether we're concerned about preparing Third World people in this country to go back home and be of help agriculturally there. We've got to be aware of that.

Flowerday: Of the foreign graduates or international graduate students that I advise, most of them feel that the sociology, anthropology kinds of courses we would teach here would have little or no bearing on what their social situation would be back home. Therefore, they say, teach me chemistry or agronomy.

B. Baker: We've had those who've said, "I would never have learned this at home." I'm thinking in particular of one student who happened to live in our building, which may be how he got in on it—hanging around John Conner for awhile—but he said he couldn't and wouldn't have gotten this perspective in his own country.

Flowerday: We teach a seminar on world food agriculture policy. Many of these foreign students are reluctant to even come because of the political implications of what might be said in their country when they go back home. We just had an Iranian student demonsration, as many of you did, and they all wore masks. I know that three of my students were down there, but we never discussed it.

Knowles: I was interested in your comment about your poor track record with students going back home. We have had some similar problems. This leads me to bring to your attention a remark that was made by the vice-chancellor of an overseas agricultural university. He said: "Under this Title XII, I hope the American university will in some way cooperate with our faculties to train our students and provide most of that training in Pakistan because, if they're trained in Pakistan—part of their formal course work could be done at a university in America, but the research for most of their period of graduate study should be in Pakistan—they'll marry there, they'll still be in their own culture, and they'll stay. Your faculty, by virtue of the fact that they may come over and work with our faculty, will not only improve the training of graduate students, but will upgrade the level of competence of the faculty over here if by no other way than by osmosis—transfer of knowledge—and also because there is a little bit of competition in this process. They don't want to be left behind in this training program." But any attempts I have made at this approach went over like a lead balloon. It just doesn't work.

G. Beran: There isn't pressure from the governments of these other countries for such programs either, because among other things books and teachers are available here, and it's more prestigious to do the study here rather than go back and do it in their own country.

Knowles: I sent a student back to Spain under this arrangement and with the agreement that they would bring me over periodically to keep track of the student's research. I've been there twice at my own expense. . . .

Stockdale: There's something about what you presented from the data of the schools that does trouble me in relation to what I was saying today. I wonder as I look—for example, at those university studies courses and the small number of students signing up for them—if maybe the biases and the inclination towards narrowness on the part of the students in land-grant colleges isn't more of a problem than I realized. At a university of ten thousand students not very many of them will be involved vocationally in agriculture. Yet we have competition among faculty members to see who gets to teach the courses that deal with world food problems, world environment problems, and so forth, and we have people from literature, philosophy, sociology, political science, economics, and geography participating.

B. Baker: (It may be a general trend). Have we gotten over the period when people were interested in other people?

G. Beran: Do you suppose, Jerry, that we excuse ourselves of any responsibility in this whole thing? That we don't recognize this as a problem anymore because we offer the course? It's up to the students if they don't take it. We're offering it, so we no longer have any responsibility for the fact that most of our students are taking a very tightly channeled curriculum.

Lundy: I just wondered how many advisers are advising students to take such courses. In a large LGU there's no reward system for the faculty for interdisciplinary teaching. The reward system is departmental, and everybody knows that, including the students.

Hadwiger: I would like to raise a small point about Title XII as it affects teaching overseas. Not being a great student of the current situation, I was terribly upset and raised the biggest fuss when the bill was first passed because it seemed they were going to select only university officials to administer it. If the universities should have vested interest in one direction, in other words, if it suits our interests to teach the students here when they should really be taught there, it would be pretty hard to change that decision. I'm still afraid I object seriously to Title XII because of the kind of built-in leadership.

Watts: How would you suggest that this situation be modified?

Hadwiger: Well, my suggestion was that they appoint to Title XII people who were knowledgeable, but people who were neither associated with nor serving as representatives of institutions. Just the opposite. It would be made up of people who could tap the institutions, work with them, be sympathetic with them, but would not be cast in the role of representatives.

Conner: Let's have a little feedback. You've aroused my curiosity.

Watts: I've been through one meeting a month for better than a year, and now we're trying to sort out some of the details of how you begin to steer and push the officials of AID into really letting the university system interact with them in a leadership role instead of limiting the university to a simple choice of project as narrow in scope as either painting the barn this week or making a bid on a fence-mending job. If you had nonuniversity representatives on those committees, you'd have people making decisions that we couldn't live with. There's an awful lot of interaction between AID and the university system right now that's frustrating. Moreover, I'm the only director of extension on either of those committees and I would say to you with all candor that the extension system does not have a majority representation on those committees. Without that, how do you get somebody who has to administer these programs and who has some involvement in past programs overseas—or current ones—in a position to interact with AID on a policy basis that makes sense? If you just go clear outside the university system I don't think you could get meaningful kinds of interaction. I don't deny the need for outside involvement; maybe there should be more. I don't believe a nonuniversity representative would understand the discussion. This would be the point I'd make. You'd have to be in the academic stream to appreciate the significance of this as an educational endeavor.

Hadwiger: I don't see quite how you dealt with the problem of interest. It just seems to me that the university passed this committee, and the universities insisted on membership on it. This is a "university law" as enacted.

Watts: As you may or may not know though, the whole foreign assistance business is now being reviewed in the Senate.

McKenzie: There were several references made throughout the evening to the position of the university community in terms of offering courses, and more things should be said about that—if not in defense, at least in clarification. In institutions in the LDCs, one of the things we tried to do was to institutionalize certain developments so that they wouldn't come and go with the coming or passing of a person, but would be a part of an institution that would go on in spite of an individual. That's one of the strengths and also one of the prob-

lems of the university system in this country. It's well institutionalized, and you don't change it overnight. It takes quite awhile to do
it, and I think that maybe the figures George Beran showed us here
represent some rather mr 'or strides.

That leads me to say a couple of other things. There is an
organization, the new International Science and Education Council,
which is an organization between the LGU and the USDA, which has
to do with coordination, cooperation, and international science and
education. The real sustaining force within that council for the last
four years has been the international training committee which deals
with the questions you're talking about here. There's also an association of directors of international ag programs in this country. And
then there is within the National Association of Land-Grant Universities a group that has cooperated to sponsor national conferences on
this subject.

Rogers: It seems to me, George, that the curricula you described
were heavily weighted toward practical problem-solving concerns. My
friends on the faculty at Cornell talk about the tension between problem solving and theoretical criticism. If you're committed to problem
solving, you're committed within a framework, within certain
parameters, and you want to be very pragmatic about what you can do
within those parameters. On the other hand there's another part of the
university tradition which is the tradition of criticism and a concern
not simply to be advocates of program and policy, but to examine and
to raise questions about them; namely, how about a course that would
raise a serious question about American imperialism or neocolonialism in the Third World? It's not going to be listed in the
catalog that way. It will be called Problems of Dependency, but I
didn't see much in the listings that would deal with problems of
dependency or a whole range of issues that would not be very practical
to get into in terms of problem solving, but that might be very important ones in terms of the educational enterprise.

G. Beran: We do offer courses in the politics of Africa, Latin
America, and we do have courses—at least one—on imperialism, colonialism. You can comment better, Don.

Hadwiger: I don't know about that particular course. We do have
a comparative governments course—one on developing countries.

Bodine: We can't really measure how much student interest there
is by how few sign up for these courses, because I think all universities
have short courses—institutes that meet for a week—and I think most
universities have some of these courses dealing with hunger, for example. You might have one hundred, two hundred, three hundred

students coming for a short course. They make a commitment for a shorter period of time.

Conner: I expect in our concluding recommendations we'll get into some of the questions of what our appropriate response should be in some of these areas; in the analysis of what is available; and also a concern about the role of the university, the church, and our relation to both.

B. Baker: I want to raise this point tonight. We've offered a course in interdependent worlds—purposefully vague—through our honors program and found that the practical colleges and the liberal arts colleges divide. The practical sort says, ''Well, if we have a problem we just need more technology and everything will be OK.'' They're still getting from somewhere—I guess it's the faculty—what has been referred to as the technological fix. All you need is a little more technology, and there's to be no asking of questions. It's the same sort of point you raised. The liberal arts students are saying, ''Maybe it's not the only way.'' I guess I'm asking what our responsibility is in the relationship to the technology being the be-all and end-all of problem solving.

Hessel: What is the commitment of persons here who are on the faculties or administrations of land-grant schools? What is your commitment to the church's network? I can see a number of places where that becomes a very interesting question. A number of you travel the world in behalf of LGU business. What is your connection to the church in that process? What disciplines ought to be operative in your work as you do that? Is there some sort of collaborative monitoring process that we could envision? Is there some common action by the CM, broadly defined to include all of us, to gain some leverage on various institutional arrangements, curriculum, and conferences?

Watts: This comment is intriguing to me personally. I raise a secondary question of procedure. If we break into groups, is there a way to get back an amalgam of ideas? What objectives do we really have here? Can we begin to structure some follow-up? We've got people within the congregation who are qualified people in their own right. To what extent could these people be used in foreign ministry I don't really know. I don't think anybody's tried to sort it out. You raised a question about our travel overseas and around this country. You know, we've never really had any way to touch base. I go bouncing off to some place like Nepal, and all I see are temples and idols, and I come back home with some knickknacks for the family. There could be some better opportunity for interaction. We'd have to have help. I, as an individual, couldn't do this unless somebody put a friendly little hand in mine, led me down the path, and shared some things you can do. "If you're really a Christian and you really want to help, take an extra day or two of your own time when you're in Taiwan or Bangladesh, and look up this missionary." I think it's got a lot of potential if we could put it together.

Conner: That's one of the options. When I was in Lahore, the missionaries were brought together—all the community development workers. It was a rich afternoon involving YWCA people, agricultural extension people, and a school principal. I hope our consultation will produce a useable manuscript, with ideas we can replicate in our own geographic areas. It would help us build in the church and in the school itself, our sense of being in the game together with others and affirming that faith and action are one.

G. Beran: When we were on the mission field in the Philippines, a project in which we were very much involved came under partial sponsorship by World Health Organization (WHO). The following summer, when we returned from the mission field, they invited us to come back, this time directly under WHO. I immediately wrote to our Presbyterian church and to the university where I had been working in the Philippines suggesting that since the project was the same, the university in the Philippines which I was with should continue to have a kind of credit as having been part of starting the project. For this reason it would be good if I could be related to the university where I had been. This was very much desired by the Philippine university, but I didn't get to first base.

Conner: If you're really interested in missions in Java, you'll go to Congress and lobby for the restoration of the AID funds for rural electrification because we've anticipated this work, and we're ready to move into some of the villages, and now the plug has been pulled. That would really be a most effective act of mission to perform for us.

Rogers: In different parts of the world, or different countries, there's a very different situation. What you have described may be true in Indonesia. In parts of Latin America, maybe most of it, the United States Embassy and AID are part of the State Department's operation, but because they are so distant from the struggle in which so many Third World Christians are involved, they are really seen as the enemy. I think the hardest thing for me in going the first time to Brazil was to realize that I had to make a choice about which side I was on. They were really very much afraid of the United States presence and the State Department, AID, and the whole establishment, so it's not an easy situation.

8 UNITED PRESBYTERIAN INVOLVEMENT IN THIRD WORLD AGRICULTURAL DEVELOPMENT

THOMAS HALLER

A MULTITUDE of different international public and private agencies are involved in agricultural development efforts related to the Third World countries. Land-grant universities represent one such group and the churches make up a second. Because this meeting centers on the relationship of the United Presbyterian Church, USA, to the LGUs and our involvement in international agricultural development, it seemed appropriate to include a consideration of the agricultural development efforts of the UPCUSA.

I examine the nature of these efforts on the part of our church in a general way. In addition some interpretive comments are made about the comparison of these efforts to those of the LGUs. Finally, I discuss several of the points at which these two efforts touch and interrelate. This treatment of the subject is not meant to be exhaustive in detail. Its intention rather is to present general insights that will help guide our discussion together.

THE NATURE OF UPCUSA EFFORTS

The first aspect of the UPCUSA effort that needs mentioning is the long history of agricultural work on the mission fields overseas. Decades before the LGUs and the other secular development agencies began their work abroad, the UPCUSA and other churches were on the scene and at work. One of the early pioneers for the UPCUSA was Sam Higginbottom whose work led to the founding of the world famous Allahabad Agricultural Institute in 1910.

Until rather recently a definite emphasis was given to the promotion of agricultural development through the founding and support of formal agricultural training institutions. Besides Allahabad Agricultural Institute in India, the UPCUSA has helped found and/or

Thomas Haller is an agricultural economist working as a consultant in Davis, California. He has served as an agricultural missionary in Africa and Latin America, and is an adviser to agricultural missions.

support other such institutions of agricultural training as the American University in Lebanon, Yonsei University in Korea, Libamba Rural Training Center in the Cameroons, and Silliman University in the Philippines. While these educational institutions are strong in the teaching area, they also sponsor programs of research and community outreach.

At the same time that much of the focus of work of the UPCUSA was on agricultural education, there has always been other less institutionalized work. Typically, this has been centered on a particular individual, or couple, who provided technical assistance, supplied modern inputs, sponsored demonstrations, and other low-cost, largely non-institutionalized forms of assistance. Often these efforts were developed on the field, as needs were identified and formally or informally integrated with other forms of community assistance.

These latter types of involvement still persist but have been reduced in number. At the same time there has been a shift to a more institutionalized approach of providing many of these same services. Centers of extension education, cooperative development, short courses, demonstration projects, and the like have come to replace the past emphasis on the formal educational institution. Examples of this type of approach are the Agape Program in Guatemala, the Northwest Project in Colombia, the Thal Development Project in Pakistan, and the Dembi Dollo Rural Project in Ethiopia. Many of these projects focus on more than agriculture and assume a more integrated rural development character.

The Thal Community Development Project extends outward from two groups of three Christian villages that are separated by 100 miles. The people, following the partition of India and Pakistan in 1947, were settled on 15-acre parcels of what is really a desert area. Fraternal workers, Mary and Lee Reed, are working with Pakistanis in land reclamation, in establishing industry, and in literacy work. Lee Reed, a trained agriculturist, oversees the grain store's seed, fertilizer, and insecticide business; the equipment rentals; and the agricultural extension programs. Well drilling, irrigation, and land leveling have enabled the farmers to upgrade and expand the land that is farmed and the crops that are produced. Rope making, carpet weaving, and embroidery are already underway as cottage industries. More phases of industrial development will be added as teachers are trained.

While the UPCUSA has steadfastly maintained its interest and involvement in agricultural development work, its direct work in agriculture has not been as extensive as that of other churches such as the Methodists and Mennonites. Historically, our major emphasis in direct social services, in general, has been on education and medicine.

However, these services become much more important in the context of the current focus that is being given to rural development as opposed to just agricultural development. The Northwest Project, in Colombia, is a current example of mission that combines programs of church development, economic life, education, and public health to enable total rural development.

There has also been a shift in the last twenty years or so away from a dependence on the UPCUSA missionary and UPCUSA founded projects. The shift to indigenizing the work of the church in agriculture began many years ago, but really took hold during the 1960s. The second type of shift has been toward the support of ecumenical programs of agricultural development through groups such as Church World Service, World Council of Churches, and Agricultural Missions. Our present commitments depend very heavily on this ecumenical approach. In fact, while our direct support of traditional Presbyterian programs has perhaps declined somewhat in the last few years, our ecumenical support of agricultural development programs currently is at a level of financial support unsurpassed in the history of the church. This is due, of course, to the impetus of the Second Development Decade and the more recent massive programming around the issue of world hunger.

Such efforts have included everything from solar-heated greenhouses in New Mexico to the development of local pumps for irrigation along the Omo River in Ethiopia; the revitalization of cattle production in Tanzania—through Heifer Project International—to a massive agricultural/community development scheme through the Development Foundation of Turkey.

Technoserve is an example of an ecumenical agency that we support. The United Presbyterian church, through its Hunger Fund, assists this nonprofit organization in its efforts to help developing nations to establish and expand enterprises which provide income for poor people. In Ghana it assists poor sugarcane farmers to obtain bank loans for working capital, crop improvements, and expansion. It provided services of evaluation, technical development, implementation, and management for a small-scale sugarcane processing plant there. Our support of the Commission on Inter-Church Aid, Refugee, and World Service (CICARWS), the relief arm of the World Council of Churches, has enabled the effort toward economic liberation in Guinea-Bussau and Cape Verde, two very poor countries isolated from other parts of the African continent. Self-sufficiency in foodstuffs and control of the environment are two goals in which we participate through the Hunger Fund. Rice production, a milk production plant, a pharmaceutical laboratory, a program of precooperative training, assistance in fishing and carpentry cooperatives, mobile health teams, and a literacy program are some of the ways communities in these two countries are beginning to develop the key sectors of their economic life: agriculture, industry, employment, health, and education.

COMPARISONS BETWEEN UPCUSA AND LGUs EFFORTS

The most striking comparisons between the efforts in agricultural development by the UPCUSA and the LGUs center on their dissimilarities. Most LGUs efforts through their AID missions are massive in comparison to those of the UPCUSA. The LGUs work almost exclusively through government channels, both through United States AID and the host country's governmental agencies. Such links are not as dominant for the UPCUSA.

At the same time similarities do exist. The emphasis on formal education and institution building are common to both. So too has been the shift toward a focus on rural development as opposed to just agricultural development. Lately the LGUs have shown renewed interest in small farmers and local community organizations. In all these specific areas, however, it is interesting to note that the church has provided the pioneering work.

RELATIONSHIPS BETWEEN THE UPCUSA AND THE LGUs

Although it is often assumed that there is a complete separation between the efforts of UPCUSA and the efforts of the LGUs, this is not the case. In the first place, most of the agricultural missionaries our chuch has sent out over the years have been products of the LGUs. At the same time these missionaries, once in the field, have looked to the LGUs for advice and information. The church in its leadership development program has provided numerous scholarships to aid Third World individuals to come to the United States and study at the LGUs.

On a different level, individual professionals from the LGUs have served the church as short-term volunteers, special consultants, and members of advisory committees. On the field, there have been numerous examples of collaboration between LGU mission staff and the staff of the church's rural projects. Finally, there are instances of formal programmatic links between overseas programs of the two agencies.

THE UNIQUENESS OF THE ROLE OF THE UPCUSA

Many of the unique features of the agricultural development effort of the UPCUSA have already been cited. However, there remain important additional features worth noting. First, one of the definite assets that the churches in general possess is the presence of thousands of local churches throughout the rural areas in the developing nations. This community-based structure provides a touchstone for programs at the local level. One of the problems that international research and development agencies have expressed is finding a viable mechanism for the dissemination of their results.

A second feature is the flexibility of the church in responding to need. This relates not only to the timeliness of response but also to the nature of the response. The churches are in a much better position than most other agencies to take on unpopular, politically sensitive, and high risk projects. One example of this is the emergency grain shipments being made to Vietnam under sponsorship of Church World Service (CWS).

A final feature that is important to mention is the recent emphasis on influencing government and business policies as they relate to agricultural development. The churches are limited in their direct development work by the amount of resources they possess both in relation to other agencies and in relation to the need. On the other hand, it has been recognized that government and business policy impact the potential of our direct rural development work. For these and other reasons the church has undertaken an advocacy, education, and mobilization role in influencing both public and business policy. ●

INFORMAL DISCUSSION

I offer a few informal concluding comments.

There are a lot of myths about what the LGUs and churches do overseas. One of my particular hangups, or contentions, is that too many of our church members and leaders really don't know what the issues are, and how the church has been at work overseas.

Before there was an LGU, before there was the Food and Agriculture Organization—of the United Nations (FAO), before the Rockefeller Fund, there was the church, and the church was overseas and at work. It pretty much had the field to itself for many years. An interpretive comment would be that this has implications for how we in the church view our work and as a result, how others view our work. We have tended to see our work in isolation. ''Yes, there may be some other people involved, but we're really there.'' The connection between what we do and what anybody else does in overseas involvement ought to receive more attention.

In the 1950s we began to assist the formation of national churches and the development of ecumenical institutions. Our church began to rely on these indigenous churches, institutions, and organizations for its method of work in rural development. Today, probably close to 95 percent of our overseas agricultural development money is funded through these channels. One of the implications is that there is a shift in decision-making responsibility. It used to be that we here in America made the decisions about the kinds of projects we would fund, who would go overseas, and with what resources. Today there is much more local determination. However, as those of you involved with funding know, the person who holds the purse strings still can determine a lot of things.

I also want to extend the comparison of work with that of the LGU. First, the LGU tends to place emphasis on research; the church is more concerned with local delivery. This differentiation is a bit exaggerated, because increasingly we have been involved with research in the church—or localized research—and the LGU is certainly doing much more than research. The question we really didn't bring up is the position of the LGU and its role overseas in policy recommendations, policy advice to governments, and the sociopolitical values that are reinforced by this advice. It is a very tricky, sensitive area that has not been appreciated and scrutinized often enough.

Secondly, there is the obvious difference in scale of efforts. Sometimes we make it sound like our denomination is really doing more than it is, with $1 million or $2 million for overseas work on hunger. I'm sure the LGUs use up about that amount on travel back and forth. So the church's efforts are not quantitatively impressive. Meanwhile, it is getting more and more expensive to implement international development programs, particularly for the LGUs. One of the advantages of shifting to ecumenical channels and relying on community based groups to do the job is that it is less costly. The cost of sending a researcher overseas for the LGU is high. I know for our church alone in 1971 it was about $25,000 a year to field an agricultural missionary. I'm sure that is is over $40,000 a year for a staff member of a LGU.

One of the strengths of the church overseas is flexibility. It has perhaps greater flexibility than any other of the aid-giving institutions. I have often been thankful that while I was with the church in Peru and Colombia, I was given a free hand in terms of answering to a whole administrative structure above me. I answered to the local people I worked with, and that made it a lot easier to do relevant work.

Also, the church is able to take on unpopular causes. I was looking over some of our recent grants. We've given some money in Chile to groups who are not working with the government, but who are working at the grass roots level with some of the problems caused by the overthrow of the Allende regime. We've sent some food aid to Vietnam, which of couse the government could not do. We've moved into Angola and Mozambique where again the government or the LGUs have yet to get involved.

So we have flexibility, and we can take on some unpopular causes, but we have limited assets. In closing, I'd like to raise some issues that are currently before the church. I act as convener for a subcommittee that meets to look over some of the policies that the UPCUSA has established for allocating our resources to overseas agricultural development, and let me point to some questions.

1. Should there be a disciplined model for the effective use of limited resources overseas? There is the shotgun method in which you hope that something will hit, and you can then identify what makes sense and put your funds behind that. Then there is selectivity, even in terms of choosing a particular country or countries to concentrate on to do an integrated job. Finally, there is some interest in more direct, bilateral church involvement. One of the negative factors of drawing back our personnel in favor of supporting ecumenical agencies is that it may make us less sensitive to things going on there. Yet we do have the option of using local people who are often quite articulate and can address the United States situation because they have been here and studied here.

2. How can we integrate our public policy advocacy in Washington with our support of development efforts abroad? We need consistency in our public policy work and in our expenditures abroad.

3. How ecumenical should we get? Do we just go through established church channels, or do we move wider, beyond the church, in cooperation with other agencies, including the land-grant colleges? Or do we limit ourselves to church organizations?

Watts: I'd like to have you elaborate just a little on your own perspective regarding your last question. I'm interested in that in terms of how the interactions might take place in the field—whether they're better left separated or whether they can be melded together.

Haller: My primary concern is for the poverty and the injustice that exists overseas and I think that the church has to look at the best way it can use its resources to achieve justice, whether it's through its own channels, whether it is going outside its own channels, using sister churches, or not using sister churches.

J. Conner: Are you saying you would keep open unilateral intervention?

Haller: That becomes a tough question because I think in actually assessing the needs, as I get the reading from people in the Third World countries, they'll tell us when they want our direct intervention. And I think we should really look to those individuals whom we know and trust to have a good sensitivity to the local situation and recognize that they can give us that reading. By the way, they aren't always leaders of the church there, but are in ecumenical or nonchurch structures. They'll usually say, "We have the people resource except in a few cases. What we need is your support in other ways."

Hessel: What are we doing to retrain key church leaders in their analysis of the hunger issue?

Haller: Are you talking about missionaries that are currently on the field?

Hessel: Yes, and also some church leaders of indigenous churches who may have a very limited perspective on the subject itself.

Haller: We have funded the Chrysalis project at the Christian Theological Seminary which will be a locus for this kind of dialogue, but not so much with American missionaries however. It's primarily with church leaders here—bringing certain select individuals from overseas and conferring at Indianapolis. I think it's worth thinking through and seeing if something more can be done.

J. Beran: Have there been times when reorientation has been done, say in Africa or Asia? So often when individual Christians are brought to our country, they regard the trip as an award for having achieved certain offices in the church. Meanwhile, those who set rural development policy may not be involved because of the nature of the selection process.

Haller: Good point. We are trying to utilize training institutions overseas, and there are some good ones. Even some of the international centers, in terms of their technical training, offer a good resource. Unfortunately, one of the problems we've had in the church—to again raise the curriculum question—is being very well trained in the particular speciality, with a lack of breadth needed to operate at a local level. Oftentimes the specialists go back; they work at the local level for awhile; but then they have the credentials to move into the ministry of agriculture, and they soon gravitate to the city, because they have not only adopted certain technical ways but also styles of life that are not consistent with living in the rural areas with the people.

J. Beran: Along with this, we have to recognize that we are not the source of all knowledge in food production, and if we are thinking of trying to help others develop agriculturally, Korea and Taiwan and other countries could be a real source of information for people from other parts of Asia. Expertise doesn't have to come just from the First World countries. There are great agricultural developments going on in many areas of the world, and I think sharing within regional groups could be very effective. Maybe this is something the church should develop a bit more; I don't know about the LGUs.

I'd like to make a comment also on comparisons between the efforts of LGUs and the church. I think it's very significant that our church, when it has sent people overseas, for the most part has arranged for them to stay for several years if not decades, but those that come under AID or LGUs stay for quite limited terms. By the nature of where they live, the salary they receive, and so on, they are on a United States system, and they are separated from the people. I think a major contributing factor to the success of church personnel overseas is their identity with the people and their length of stay. We must not lose sight of this, particularly as we see the church sending people for short-term or volunteer work. It takes a while to get to know what is needed.

Haller: Also much preparation, language study, and cultural understanding. The church has been pretty good in that area.

Rogers: Earlier you referred to Chile, a country where United States agencies certainly helped to subvert and overthrow the government. You're in contact with church leaders in the Third World and particularly in Latin America. Are they sending any messages to us about the way we hinder their development?

Haller: Just after I left Kenya, the head of the Presbyterian church there met with the All African Council of Churches and passed a moratorium on missionaries being sent to Africa. When I went to Latin America, they called for almost the same kind of thing soon after I was there. I don't know if it was just me personally, or whether the problem was broader. There are some very understandable reasons for demanding a moratorium. I wouldn't want to see a blanket moratorium. I think there are places, times, and people that can be very effective and mutually useful. I think the social interchange must continue. I do agree that there are not many places left for North American missionaries in Latin America. In Africa the picture may be a little different.

Rogers: To follow up on that opinion. I was not talking so much about missionaries, though certainly those remarks go for missionaries too, but about Unites States development programs in Latin America.

Haller: That's true, too. The United States Agency for International Development must move, as the church has, to an acceptance and trust of indigenous groups to use our money wisely. So USAID has to move toward greater trust of some of the countries. But again, you get into a selectivity process of which countries to favor.

Carlson: It seems like one of the things LGUs could do is not to antagonize countries—by helping to train their people, rather than coming in with an all-knowing attitude. We sometimes forget that training has a more immediate impact than research assistance, for it usually takes a very long time to get research started.

Haller: Let me give you an example of shifting the decision making. When I was in Colombia, there was a Harvard Mission—a very prestigious group funded by USAID to work with a planning organization. A team of about eight people were involved at different levels—agricultural, industrial, and the like. It turned out that when the Colombian government read the fine print after two years, the Colombian government was paying an increasing proportion of the bill for the mission there. Finally they sat down, and they said, "We don't want it. It's costing us too much for what we get." What they did do was to invite one person back. They had a particular need for expertise. The valuable thing was that it put the decision-making power in their hands. When they determine what they need, the advice they receive is going to be utilized. One of the problems in technical missions many times is that the idea is conceived by the sending mission; they may even get the verbal nod of the government, but it's not a real commitment. I recall the North Carolina mission in Peru which spent many years of work down there, institutionalizing the university, sending people away for training, and spending money. When I got there, there were two faculty members and some graduate students who wanted training, but there was nobody to teach them. So the institution-building function just fell on its face, primarily because there wasn't a commitment by the government, and a realistic look at that possibility by the original mission that went there.

G. Beran: What you're saying certainly applies to lot of what's happening to missionaries going abroad. Certainly these missionaries, going and coming back to the United States and leaving the field, have been the missionaries who have been in charge of things. There are missionaries now being invited back to these countries under different circumstances—to work under the guidance of the local church or the local church-related school. We in the land-grant colleges certainly have a significant role to play in the training of these people. In our life on the mission field you could just go down the line talking to missionaries. "Where did you graduate?" "I graduated from Iowa State, or Purdue, or Cornell." So many of our land-grant colleges have been the source of these missionaries. Even though we in the Presbyterian church are sending relatively few missionaries in agriculture, this is certainly not true of many of what we call the rather small denominations or even the sect groups in this country. I get many such students coming to me and saying, "What courses shall I take in preparing to go into the mission field. I want to go under a Baptist church, or under some group of this kind." These students gravitate into our interdisciplinary food issues courses. So we do have a real role to play with them in the land-grant schools.

Knowles: In principle, in some AID programs, they try to adopt a procedure where, in the host country, you have an understudy or counterpart who will absorb everything you know and you can go home, having worked yourself out of a job. To what extent in Presbyterian supported rural development programs abroad, in the past or now, is that sort of principle applied?

Haller: It's been applied with varying success. The difficulty becomes the transference of whatever you're trying to transfer. It's a naive assumption that the person sitting next to you, following some of the things you do, is just going to learn from you and be able to carry on from you. I see all kinds of problems with that model. There have been some successes. The model we've moved to is to let the local organization identify the leader they want to work with them and then design or show them the options for training, some of the implications of that training, and let them select the option. So they're in control a little bit more, and it's not an either/or kind of situation with a lot of requirements, such as coming to the States.

Geller: We have an informal system at our university that works this way: The students with money from other countries are generally the ones we accept. That means that right now half of our foreign students are from the Organization of Petroleum Exporting Countries (OPEC). The other aspect of our system is that we've been able to interest the churches of our city in providing scholarships or accommodations for refugee students, but not for any others. But the refugees seldom go back. Locally we seem to fit into the system; we provide for those that already have the money to buy it.

Haller: Our objective must be to help development take place in these countries without having to transfer scarce resources. Educational opportunities and educational systems should be constructed in those countries consistent with their needs and their personnel, so that people do not have to come to this country and depend on our resources. There are many more positive things about that model, though you can't jump to it immediately. There has to be a strategy to achieve it.

9 CLASHING OVERVIEWS: NEED FOR NEW SOLUTIONS TO HUNGER

WILLIAM W. ROGERS

THE OTHER DAY I was asked to speak to a world hunger seminar on the topic, "An Overview of the World Hunger Problem." It seemed important to point out in the lecture that there are competing overviews of the hunger problem, and that we may have to make a choice between them. For, apart from offering immediate relief in emergency situations, we may need to do very different things in the pursuit of long-term solutions to world hunger—especially in relation to the Third World—depending on which assessment of the problem we choose. I thought it might be helpful to contrast those choices.

OVERVIEWS

The Liberal/Conservative Consensus
The prevailing overview of the world hunger problem in the churches and universities of the United States is, I would say, a corollary of Western economic liberalism. Economic liberalism holds that human needs will best be served by a global, free-enterprise system of efficient production and untrammeled commerce. In this view, the hunger problem stems from the fact that world population, especially in the food-deficient countries, is expanding geometrically, while agricultural production is progressing, at best, arithmetically. The system simply can't keep up.

What is seen are two parallel escalators. The one, population growth, is outstripping the other, the growth of food production. The trick—simply—is to slow the one to the speed of the other; then gradually reduce the acceleration of each to zero.

If we can just do that, then everyone will have a chance to have enough. Detractors, of course, point out that the problems of

William W. Rogers was United Ministries in Higher Education Campus Minister, Cornell University, Ithaca, New York.

distribution are not to be passed over so lightly. But most North Americans, and especially academics in the hard sciences, are likely to be impatient with that objection. "Look," they say, "if science and technology can solve the problem of food production (and birth control), then surely the politicians can solve the problems of distribution."

Typically those of this persuasion regard distribution problems as problems of corruption. Why don't Nigerian peasants get their share of the food aid given their country? Dishonest politicians. Corrupt officials. Irritating problems, to be sure, but nothing compared to the challenges undertaken by the academics. "If we can develop miracle strains of rice and wheat, and better means of birth control, surely the 'soft' sciences can break the logjams of petty politics."

Dissonance from the Third World

An alternative "overview" comes to us with increasing force from the Third World. As I hear the message, these men and women are saying to us that the problem of hunger is a problem of economics. Hungry people are poor people, and poor people are hungry, quite simply, because they are not "markets." As long as food is regarded as a commodity to be sold to the highest bidder then, clearly, the rich will eat and the poor will go hungry. It doesn't matter whether a country produces a lot of food, or whether it is densely or thinly populated. What matters is whether you have money. Saudi Arabia may be a desert, and Denmark may be overpopulated, but the Saudis and the Danes are not hungry—because they've got money. The points is that in this view, world hunger is the result of poverty, not dense populations nor underproduction.

Examples

Two Caribbean islands are frequently cited as cases in point.

Cuba. Since the revolution of 1969, Cuba has virtually eliminated the problem of endemic hunger, along with a number of the other most poignant symptoms of poverty (malnutrition, illiteracy, and disease, among the most basic). How did Cuba do it? By means of social organization. The Cuban government—the "Revolution," they would say—put the needs of the people (read "poor") as its number one priority. No one was to be left out. Everyone was to have access, as resources would allow, to food, medicine, education, housing, and recreation.

There was a price to be paid. We all know that. Most of the rich, and the professionals who served them, left the country. Not all, but most. Per capita income fell. "Productivity," at least in the early stages of the revolution, suffered. But the grinding hunger of the marginalized poor came to an end. Some say that after the revolution everyone became poor. Men and women had to stand in line for their rations—for food, medical care, and an evening at the "Tropicana." But nobody starved. Everyone had a ration book. Some say everyone became rich. Ernesto Cardenal, a Nicaraguan monk, called it the richness of the monastery.

An economist friend of mine at Cornell remarked one evening that Cuba was an economic failure. By what standard? I wondered. "If you were a peasant *(campesino),* would you rather live in Brazil (with its "economic miracle") or in Cuba?" "If I were a peasant," he said, "I'd rather live in Cuba, but I'm not a peasant—and none of my friends are—and, given your question, I'd rather live in Brazil." An honest statement which, he would admit raises the question: "failure" and "miracle" for whom?

Dominican Republic. But take the case of the Dominican Republic. As part of the "Free World" the Dominican Republic is open to foreign investment and entrusts the development of its agriculture to the hands of the global corporations, USAID, and the North American universities. Enter the liberals with their twin escalators. Step up food production at any (well, almost any) cost, and push birth control—or "family planning," as the demographers now call it—with all the ingenuity the social scientists can muster.

The story is familiar.

Agribusiness groups like Gulf and Western come in, buy up much of the best farmland, and through capital-, energy-, and technology-intensive farming boost the production of food to the profit of the corporations and a few local elites, but at the expense of the Dominican workers and their families. Why? If food production goes up in the Dominican Republic, why don't the Dominicans have more and eat better?

The answer is simple. What's produced is not food for hungry (poor) Dominicans, but "commodities" (sugar and beef) for the international market—for United States breakfast tables and fast-food chains. So we have the apparent paradox of rising food production and, at the same time, increasing poverty, malnutrition, and hunger. Only it's not a paradox at all. As long as the Dominican Republic is treated (and allows itself to be treated) as an open resource to be exploited by powerful international corporations for the benefit of a wealthy and powerful foreign state, it will, ipso facto, continue to produce a Dominican society split between wealthy collaborators at the top and a hungry and repressed majority throughout the countryside and in the city slums. There's no mystery about this.

Recapitulation

So, as we are doubtless all aware, there are competing "overviews" as to what the world hunger problem is.

The Twin Escalators. One view, the liberal-conservative consensus, that fits in nicely with United States interests and especially with the interests of its global corporations, big foundations, international banks, and colleges of agriculture, sees the world in terms of the twin escalators: Third World countries are hungry because their agricultural production is low and their birthrates are too high. Problem: Third World peoples are backward, short on money and technology, and have too many babies. Solution: send help from the outside in the form of bank loans, corporate investments, modern management, academic advisors, and United States-sponsored programs of population control and "public safety." Step up the production of everything the foreign corporations can mine, grow, and manufacture; do what you can (it won't be much) about "family planning"; celebrate any rise in the "per capita income"; and beef up the army and civil police to discourage any protest from the "capita" who don't get their share. Hope that someday there will be enough "leftovers" from the feast of the few to cure the famine of the multitude.

Oppression. The other view from the Third World—which seems to threaten United States interests, and especially the interests of its global corporations, big foundations, international banks, and colleges of agriculture—sees the world hunger problem as the result of a deadly contest between the rich minorities of the world (in the United States a majority), and the overwhelming power of the institutions through which they exercise their will—and the world's impoverished majorities, who are effectively prevented from organizing their own interests and are consequently robbed of their natural resources. Problem: Third World peoples are oppressed. They are vulnerable to the intrusions of Western economic and military power (often in the guise of domestic economic and military institutions) and are impoverished by transnational systems which exploit their natural resources and defenseless labor. Solution: Change the social structures which perpetuate these injustices. Overturn the national elites (often military) who sell out the country. Expel the foreign exploiters and organize the country for the benefit of the hungry majorities.

IMPLICATIONS FOR THE CAMPUS MINISTRY

A. N. Whitehead once said that any simplification is an oversimplification. These overviews, as stated here, are obviously too simple. Each is the tip of an iceberg. The issues between these contrasting viewpoints are deep and incredibly complex. Yet to say that an issue is stated too simply is not to say that it has no correspondence with the truth.

What are the implications of all this for the CM?

I think there is a challenge to the whole Church to begin to approach the world hunger problem (or, let's say, the world poverty problem) in a much more ecumenical and prophetic manner. Up until now we have largely reinforced the liberal overview. This overview, shared by conservatives as well as liberals in our churches, is very much the product of our Western, Protestant, middle-class heritage—and of our recent, North American experience.

To approach the problem more ecumenically means to be open to a genuinely international and interclass dialogue. The rich (we middle-class North Americans) must learn to listen to and be instructed by the poor of the earth, and by those who live in genuine solidarity with them.

To approach the problem prophetically means not only to share the prophetic passion for justice, but to share the prior concern of the biblical prophets about the worship of false gods. I am convinced that what prevents us from entering this dialogue, more than anything else, is our fear of "communism." There has been no "end of ideology" in the United States, though it serves our interests enormously to pretend that there has. I believe that there does indeed exist a powerful, American middle-class ideology that is thoroughly mixed with the popular religiosity of our churches, and like the worship of Baal, makes no connection between religious devotion and the pursuit of righteousness.

There is an evangelical and pastoral task to be done. It is to untangle our liberal ideology from the historic, biblical faith of the Church, and give people in our churches the chance to make a clear choice: first, to be disciples of the Servant Lord Jesus—then, in light of that commitment, to decide on which side of the United States/Third World split we ought to stand.

CONCLUSION

I have always thought that Christian students, and to some extent the professors and campus ministers who support them, should be the "forward scouts" of the Church. Like Joshua and Caleb in the days of the Exodus, they should, at times, move far ahead of the wandering Israelites—sometimes even beyond the boundaries of class and nation—exploring the terrain the community of faith must someday encounter. And like these ancient scouts, we and our students must also return from the land of the strangers and share our ex-

periences, our questions, and our hopes with the Children of Israel—
for it may be that the fearful Land of Canaan may also be a land of
promise.   ●

INFORMAL DISCUSSION

Rogers: In the summer of 1965 I went as codirector of what we
then called the Cornell/Brazil project, into a peasant village in Northeast Brazil where we were joined by a larger number of students of the
Brazilian Student Christian Movement to undertake a work camp.
The Brazilian students insisted that they be in the majority because
that was their turf, and they wanted it to be their project if they did it
at all. These were the early years of the Alliance for Progress and of
the Peace Corps. But the students didn't believe that the Alliance for
Progress was there to do them any good. They didn't believe that
foreign investments being lured into Brazil were going to help poor
people.

These students were afraid of Americans because they knew better than we did what United States interests in Brazil really were, and
they weren't to help poor people. The military came down very hard
on them. The students were very much committed to the left which is
another way of saying they were committed to the struggles of the
peasant, of the poor, of the slum dweller. Now, the Student Christian
Movement in Brazil doesn't even exist. The military police simply
broke it up; invaded their offices. Many of those students with whom
we worked that summer have been dragged through the torture pits of
Brazil. I sat up all night with one young doctor who had been a student of our project. Because some students had been in his apartment
and the secret police were pursuing students, he was tortured badly
just to get information.

I think there's been something lacking in our consultation. We
haven't talked very much about the cost of the kind of development
that we have been encouraging in the Third World—namely, development within the international capitalist system.

When I spent a sabbatical year (1968–1969) in Brazil, I wrote an
analysis about my reason for living there a year and talking to hundreds of people. It was to try to understand what development meant
in Brazil; how students, priests, bishops, factory workers, and others
felt about what was going on, who was benefitting, who was being left
out.

What does it mean for North American universities and churches
to be promoting development projects, including agricultural development, within that kind of society? Brazil is now producing more

agricultural products than ever before, but hunger is more widespread—there are more starving children in northeast Brazil than there were ten years ago. Most of the product increase is export commodities like soybeans and coffee. We need to deal with not only the problem of hunger, but with the issue of poverty and, as the Brazilians would say, with the issue of oppression.

One of the most powerful forces coming out of Latin America today is a movement within the Roman Catholic Church—the Theology of Liberation. Its origins can be traced to a close contact of priests, sisters, lay people, and bishops with the very poor of Latin America. In 1968 the bishops of Latin America met in Colombia to talk about what was happening in Latin America. The Bishops said, "We're not underdeveloped in Latin America, we're oppressed." This was a different way of conceiving what the problem was, and it implied a very different program of action. The Theology of Liberation is fundamentally about the reality of opposition to oppression, and it's one of the most powerful, reforming, theological movements in the world.

We need to be hearing from that theology in the American church and that view raises one of the questions I have about our consultation here. Why, when we come together as Christians to talk about hunger in the Third World, don't we invite brothers and sisters from the Third World, who are also deeply concerned about that problem and deeply concerned about the interconnection, to share their concerns?

One of the things we really must do—and the church with our university colleagues can do that better—is to make sure that these people do meet with us and that we learn to listen to them. I suppose that if I had anything to lay before this group it would be that Third World friends who are speaking clearly to us about the structures of oppression are people we need to be close to, listen to, and to have in our midst. Gustavo Guitterrez, a Jesuit in Lima, Peru, says to us North Americans, "We're not saying you should get involved in politics; we're saying you should change sides. We know you're involved, but you don't know the degree to which you are involved."

In our international project at Ithaca, Americans' lack of awareness of the depth of our involvement became clearer to us as we tried to respond to the Chilean crisis and bring Chilean refugees to Ithaca. We got people from the churches in Ithaca together—Catholics and Protestants—and we said, "Will you help us bring a refugee from a Chilean prison?" they said, "Hold on a minute, who are these people? Aren't they in prison because they are socialists supporting Allende? Isn't the new government friendly to us?"

"Yes, that's true."

"You're getting us involved in politics by asking us to help bring socialists and Marxists to Ithaca."

"We must do this for humanitarian reasons."

"No, it's really political isn't it?"

"We think we need to hear what they have to say about what our country did in Chile."

While this was going on at an agonizing level, the war ended in Vietnam and without asking anyone, pastors in our churches said, "For humanitarian reasons we must respond immediately to the plight of the Vietnamese." This stunned the people who were trying to help Chilean refugees. Nobody raised any political questions about the Vietnamese. Why? Because they were on our side.

We work in churches and universities which are deeply, subconsciously committed politically. The challenge for us is to see that commitment, to step backward, and then to reconsider what we are doing.

Bodine: Why has the radical, political movement arisen in the Roman Catholic Church and not among the Protestants who are in Latin America?

Rogers: It's not that it hasn't happened in the Protestant churches, but the Protestant churches tend to become very closed. In Brazil, for example, the Presbyterian church is made up, to a large extent, of people who one or two generations ago were very poor. Partly because of the literacy training of the Presbyterian church of Brazil, the members acquire skills that help them rise to the lower levels of the emerging middle class. That's where the leadership of the Presbyterian church is. It's very insecure. They remember the poverty. It's a different life after they become lower-level civil servants, military officers, businessmen, or professionals. This group of people has become very anticommunist. They are scared to death of the left. Any who become committed to the poor in their student movement days simply find themselves at a dead end. A whole generation of students from the Student Christian Movement is just out of the church because they couldn't go anywhere. It didn't happen in the Catholic church, partly because the Catholic church is big. It has its conservative side, but also its very liberal wing. Dom Helder Camara is the best example. There are a number of bishops like him. I think they've gone that direction because more than any other educated people they're in contact with the poor, but they're not threatened by the poor in the same way Protestants are.

Bodine: Why are they not threatened? Is it because they're single and have no families?

Rogers: I don't mean that the personal threats aren't there. The priests, even nuns, have been tortured and jailed. I think it's a deeper, cultural thing. They've always been part of the majority. They're not marginalized the way Protestants are. They're not seeking their place in the sun. I'm not sure I can explain it much beyond that.

Gittings: In Latin America the Protestants are a class church. The Catholic church exists in every strata of society—a true cross section.

Carlson: I'd like to go a little further into this assertion you make about oppression. I've not lived or been in Brazil, but I've read about it, especially some of the economic studies. As I understand it, they've used many different mechanisms and export duties. They've used tier pricing to funnel out money from the agricultural sectors to other sectors. If we talk of this only as oppression rather than the economic mechanisms by which it's being done, I think we miss part of the picture. I think we need to understand those markets and how they're being manipulated. Those people in the rural areas have to be trained to understand what's going on, why prices are so high, why they are so badly off relative to the people of São Paulo, why they can't have an automobile. That's partly an educational task, and it has to be a very big part of any effort in rural areas. If we just point fingers of blame and don't come through with some positive things, it sounds very dismal, and I don't think it has to be that way. What do you see wrong with the market system as a way for these people to build up their livelihood?

Rogers: Brazil is run by a military government which prides itself on being modern. They rely very much on economists trained in North American universities. They have done a remarkable thing with their neoclassical economics backed up by military power; any policy that is decided to be the right one, the military can enforce. The military elites are committed to the middle and upper classes which might be 20 percent of the population, largely urban and committed to a world-power status. They want a state that will not only produce cars, televisions, and refrigerators, but one that can produce tanks, jets, and missiles. The technocrats say they can't be worried about poor people or their state of development. I think it's myopic to suppose that they will join an international capitalist system so well capitalized and so well run that the poor will have some meaningful share.

Carlson: If rural people are trained, they learn how to use their markets; they learn what is being done to them. In terms of taking out of the rural sector all the export earnings and using it in other economic sectors, it's just one economic group oppressing another economic group through manipulation of prices. But we've not been able to come in on the other side and show the agriculturalists what they can do. I'm not so sure I'm ready to throw everything out just because one group has learned how to use economic mechanisms better than the other.

Rogers: It's not my purpose to try to prescribe what Brazil ought to do. What I know is that the United States is deeply involved there in every aspect of Brazilian life. Nelson Rockefeller after his fact-finding mission said, "You wouldn't believe the extent to which we're telling the Brazilians how to do everything." He was right.

Stockdale: I've talked to a lot of anthropologists and social scientists and others who have been in Latin American countries and what you're saying rings very true in terms of what I've been hearing from them.

In many places there is a problem of oppression and a problem of underdevelopment; often the two are linked together. Oppression is the cause of underdevelopment for particular segments of the society. If we look at Latin America, we do well to emphasize the oppression. If we look at South Africa, we do well to emphasize oppression. If we look at Tanzania and some of the other countries in the developing world, we do well to emphasize the underdevelopment, but even there, if we want to understand how the countries got to be where they are, we must remember a long history, first of political and later of economic colonialism. And so I find your remarks especially helpful because they so forcefully state the point on oppression and its relation to underdevelopment.

Ryan: As a footnote to this dialogue, I want to raise some basic questions that maybe we've overlooked about justice within the United States. I'm probably one of the few people in the room who is not institutionally connected either with the land-grant college or the church, so I have a slightly different perspective, and I find myself in a pretty unusual place in advocating something of a conservative position.

I would like to urge us to draw back and look critically at the structures we're talking about dealing with. In coming together like this we're responding to a push to broaden the mandate of the land-grant colleges. In the last ten years, a lot of us have talked about broadening the mandate beyond serving the needs of the people in this country to serving the needs of people all over the world. I'd like us to ask ourselves and the land-grant college system—whether we teach there or are connected with ministries there—how effective we really have been in meeting the needs of the people in this country. I have a bias. I don't think we have been effective. I travel around the United States a lot and I see struggling farmers in the South, in Appalachia, and the Northeast. I see people in the inner cities in this country that don't have access to good food, and that raises some very basic questions for me about the methods of production we presently use in this country.

Unquestionably the land-grant complex has been very successful. It's probably the most influential agricultural research complex in the world. We'll be spending about 3 or 4 billion tax dollars combined with corporate monies this year on agricultural research and extension. Yet somehow the word that keeps coming to my mind is accountability. I think we are all individually concerned with the question of accountability.

One of the problems with the agricultural research systems in this country as I perceive the situation is that there are no clear lines of accountability and there are no clear mechanisms for setting policy. The task in many ways before us in the next five or ten years, as we move into other areas, is to consider why we have not been as effective as we'd like to have been and what we can do about it. We can examine critically the kinds of priorities we have and the way we set those priorities. This calls for some basic structural change within the land-grant complex.

I direct the Responsible Agricultural Project in Washington. We're starting an independent research program in five states to examine what in fact these priorities are and to identify the kinds of things we can do to begin to tie into that system certain constituencies who have been overlooked in the past fifty years.

10 NEXT STEPS FOR CHURCH AND UNIVERSITY

FOLLOWING the dialogue found in the preceding chapters, the participants in the Informal Consultation on the Response of Land-Grant Universities to World Hunger moved into four subgroups to formulate recommendations on: "new" agriculture, United States foreign assistance, curriculum reform, and the implications for the Campus Ministry.

Reports of subgroups on "new" agriculture, curriculum reform, and strategic implications for the CM appear below as presented by participants to the concluding plenary session. Concerns pertinent to the subject of the subgroup on United States foreign assistance are summarized, because a verbatim report was not possible.

The recommendations were received, rather than adopted by formal action of the participants, since the consultation was not intended to be a policy-setting body. Some of the recommendations are mere indications of the participants' concerns; others are quite specific, next-step suggestions, all of which should be evaluated for their intrinsic merit. Implementation of these recommendations is the responsibility of individual participants, a follow-up task force of UMHE, and of the hunger programs of the churches and of university groups.

"NEW" AGRICULTURE
a report by Gerald Carlson

Our group was charged to look at alternative agriculture. We have a long list of descriptors for "new," or more appropriate agriculture. We considered briefly the impediments to the implementation of "new" agriculture, and we offer some specific recommendations for action by LGUs and the church.

The "new" agriculture is not a technological fix; there are some other components to it. It's a combination of new technological developments and new forms of organization and institutions to which social scientists and others can contribute.

Descriptors of a "New" Agriculture

Providing opportunities for small family farms in the United States and overseas. One focus of LGUs is to work on problems that will help a lot of people, and certainly there are a lot of small family farms, so that has to be a primary focus.

Self-sufficiency. There's a lot of disagreement about what this means, but we feel strongly that some countries and some regions have to be looking toward ways of not being so vulnerable to these ups and downs of energy shortages, commodity prices, and concessional sales.

Transpolitical approach. We want to transcend the ideological boundaries in developing new technologies. If it happens creatively in a socialist country or wherever, we want to be looking for these developments and not let our society's preference for a mixed-capitalist economy fix our ideas on that approach.

New marketing mechanisms. This turns out to be very important when food gets produced but doesn't get delivered to those who need it most. We favor local market mechanisms, storage facilities, and roadside marketing. Here in the United States we welcome a move-ment toward reduced dependency on that nonfood component of the food cost in the supermarket. What are the new market mechanisms, contracts, futures markets, and co-ops?

Support for limited resource farmers. These are the people who have been left behind. There was an important study 10 to 15 years ago in this country about the people left behind—limited resource people, people without opportunities—and certainly we have to design things for them. What can agricultural scientists do for low-skill farmers in agriculture? They can train more talented young people in the United States in agricultural sciences; train more foreign students for international agricultural research; train United States farmers, especially those with little formal education; and develop technologies for low-skill farmers.

Less energy- and capital-intensive agriculture as well as conserva-tion of natural resources. Sylvan Wittwer's discussion (chap. 3) con-cerns these issues.

Alternative means of production. These are different ways of viewing this concept. One view is that you are hanging in a willow tree (Don Hadwiger's analogy) and you somehow have to get over to a new system, a new tree. It's a very difficult move. We're talking here about various organic systems—integrated pest management systems, short season crops that reduce stresses, and genetic systems.

Maximize participation by numbers of people in the production and marketing of food, especially in the Third World. This is similar to promoting the small family farm. We want to direct LGU research toward those things that happen to involve a lot of people. If people are producing food, they're not going to be as hungry as if they have to depend on someone far away.

Providing sufficient, nutritious food to all people.

Providing more agricultural jobs. The problem is not just lack of food, but it is also one of poverty, and we have to have income for people to buy food if they're not producing it directly.

Increasing the skills of agricultural workers. There is a big educational component to this: We can never look toward self- determination in the Third World unless we get some training there in production, safety, and public health.

Increased bargaining power. There are several forms of unions, co-ops, and other bargaining groups through which farmers can get their wishes across to the consumers. We also mentioned the need for consumer education.

Optimum involvement of women. Women are important in fostering the nutrition of the family by deciding what gets cooked; and in many places they are the producers on the farm, because the male tends to work off the farm. So there's a crucial role for women in the "new" agriculture, and we ought to emphasize the impact of the various approaches on women.

Impediments

I raise just two. One is that research has dropped from the priorities of the LGU system because of static faculty numbers and rising enrollments. Research gets left behind in favor of teaching. There's a shortage of people in the universities to do this research.

A second impediment is a misunderstanding between consumers and producers. There's a real gap between the consumers and the producers. Producers just don't make the connection between a short crop and hungry people. Consumers don't make the connection between low prices in this country and reduced incentives to produce. The National Council of Churches has been working on dialogues between producers and consumers, so that urban people begin to understand the problems of rural people and vice versa.

Recommendations for Action

We concluded with some specific recommendations for LGUs and churches.

1. Those who do technical research in the LGU must become more accountable for their actions. Physical and biological scientists

work on technological improvements but they seldom examine the social implications of mechanization, or the ecological implications of a new chemical. Somehow we have to reorganize within the university to look more critically at this problem of moral and public accountability.

2. One of the ideas that came up is the proposal that the LGUs, together with the churches, help change the reward system within the university for doing this type of "new" agricultural research. One suggestion (I believe by Don Hadwiger) is a system of awards. We have the soybean producers, the pork producers and others, giving awards to university people for doing a good job related to their area. What's wrong with the church having small awards for research in "new" agriculture, for developing the intermediate technology, or for small farm assistance. I think that has great appeal and it may not be too costly for what it will accomplish.

3. There has to be the political basis for research support. Certainly the church has a role there through its contacts with legislators and administrators. A caution to consider is how to keep church support of LGU research from being tokenism. It's so easy to say, "Here's a pet project of the church; we'll set a little money aside."

4. Another suggestion would be for the church to hire a food advocate to work in Washington, helped and assisted in technical areas by LGU people. This person could be related to the Interreligious Task Force on United States Food Policy. Criteria for use of a lot of the Hunger Fund money in self-development should relate to this policy as much as possible. Initiative must come from the church. A church-based task force was mentioned for carrying out and organizing this policy.

5. One of the problems talked about was what to do with and for foreign students, who are not getting back into their society and are not working on problems related to their home countries. One suggestion was to utilize more fully the international research centers, to help with thesis research. Some people are using that now, but not frequently. Students should go back to their own countries and work on their problems, using the international research centers. A point along with this is overtraining or trying to make Ph.D.'s out of these people; perhaps some other degree programs, designed for their problems, would be better.

6. We suggest that campus ministers participate in such programs as the Junior Year Abroad and travel in these developing areas with university students and faculty, to see better the problems and to sensitize different groups.   ●

INFORMAL DISCUSSION

Miner: I can't sit here as a member of an LGU and allow you to say that persons in agriculture need to become transpolitical, develop projects with less energy and less capital, less and conservation consciousness. I think these people are very aware that these resources are now in shorter supply than they used to be, and that projects now do take these facts into consideration. I don't think they are as far behind in these areas as you've implied. Moreover, you said that agricultural research persons do not always understand the implications of their projects. That proposition is kind of two-sided. In one way, yes, that's why they chose them. They're looking ahead not only at the results but the implications. In short, in true research you do not always know what every implication is going to be. I don't think you want to say that every research project has to comprehend all the implications. That's almost impossible to do.

Carlson: I think it's good to raise that point. It wasn't so much that people weren't trying, but rather that in our specialized disciplines, an entomologist, for example, goes out and develops a pest management program and doesn't think about what that's going to do to jobs elsewhere. Or the ag engineer comes up with a new mechanization process, but does not ask what that does to labor displacement. That's the sort of thing we want to overcome.

Miner: I think they're very aware of labor displacement in ag engineering. That's what they're there for.

Carlson: Do ag engineers do research on the utilization of human beings?

Miner: No, but they think about how much effort is necessary in each step.

Watts: I think the ag engineers are the people who should go back to the farm.

Carlson: Someone suggested that all we need are more social scientists, and certainly that's not the answer either. But it certainly is a component. We have specialists in labor in these social scientists, and I say that ought to be a component. We need to get more extensive dialogue going between people who are developing this "new" agriculture and the others who are studying the implications of it.

Bodine: I think one of the things we were talking about is the way the land-grant school is set up as an institution. Now it is very difficult for professors to work together interdepartmentally in research, unless they get some large amounts of money that allows them this privilege.

Miner: Virtually every dean, administrator of extension service, or director of ag experiment stations is terrifically interested in interdisciplinary projects. This is a stated goal, and they are working in as many ways as they can to implement this.

Hadwiger: If those are their goals, what we're saying is, "That's terrific; now come through as helpfully as you can in various ways in achieving them." I don't think this necessarily involves saying that they don't have the goals. It was our assumption all along that there is a great verbal willingness to pursue the "new" agriculture and also a lack of support for that kind of thing from some college administrators—possibly from most of them. More active support is something the church groups, and all the rest of us as individuals, can advocate.

C. Baker: Can I ask what transpired in your discussion regarding the use to be made of the international research centers?

Carlson: We didn't get into that topic very much. Where we did talk about them was with respect to graduate student training. We didn't talk much about organization or organizational forms for doing this research.

C. Baker: There's a gross difference among staff and what they can do.

Carlson: We noted that it would be nice if they would take on some of the training function, but they're primarily research centers and they have limited resources too.

G. Beran: In this kind of proposal we are not inferring something that's really brand new. Our universities have research going right now in these areas, along with many other areas, but what we are saying is that these are areas which we consider to be very important, that emphasis should be placed on these, and that within the framework of what we are doing, these should be areas in which we place a great deal of emphasis. I take it you don't mean to imply that these actions are not being taken and therefore we are suggesting entirely new departures.

Carlson: That's a good point, and it was discussed. The point is that there are a lot of demands on LGU personnel. If they're going to do a lot of this sort of research, they're going to slight some other things, like commercial agriculture research. And that takes some explaining by deans to some commercial agriculture people about why they aren't doing the kind of research they used to be doing. There are some trade-offs here, I think. If we intend to emphasize this aspect, then we're going to have to be supported by our administrations.

Ryan: There's a third party that really needs to be brought in here, especially if we're talking about the "new" agriculture, namely, the many community organizations which are in some ways performing the functions of land-grant colleges. They're doing their own research, their own training, their own extension, and increasingly they are networking themselves. I'd like to see the land-grant colleges and churches relate to such groups as: the Center for World Affairs in Nebraska, the Land Institute in Kansas, the Ground Center in North Carolina, and the Small Farm Project in Maine. I could name at least twenty-five similar organizations off the top of my head.

They're doing research on the problems of the small producer; they're trying to get that research out to the people. In terms of the small amount of money they have, I think their impact is enormous. They're beginning to develop an expertise and a language of their own. Many of the people involved with those organizations are graduates of the land-grant colleges, and they feel that creating their own organizations is more supportive of "new" agriculture research than working at a land-grant college.

Knowles: I feel that this report has been too negative about the accomplishments of the land-grant colleges over a period of a century. I for one am extremely proud that I am a part of that organization and that it has permitted this country to have such a small component of its society involved in farming, allowing the farmer to feed something like fifty-five people whereas in modern Russia it's only five or seven people. So I feel that this report should state that the land-grant system has accomplished a great deal for this country.

Second, I think you have to be very careful about what you call this emphasis. You say it's "new" agriculture, but in a sense, you're talking about an agriculture centuries back in our economy, and you have to be precise about what you mean by a "new" agriculture. The way part of it is phrased now, you're implying that we should go back a century in time and farm that way.

I have mixed feelings about "making jobs." Farms should make more jobs, as should all of the components of society. Set up your banks so they won't use computers—do it by hand—then you can make jobs. I don't think you should single out farming necessarily to make jobs, because you're talking in terms of low salaries for people on farms when you do that. I'm negative to recommendations that you make jobs on farms, per se. You should have efficient farmers and laborers on farms so you can pay them well.

Watts: Your recommendations seem to be completely research oriented. I've got to put my biases against that bias and say that there's an extension component in here that ought not to be ignored. You are not going to use research without developing some kinds of distribution patterns and ideas. I hate to see that missed.

Gibson: It's important to remember that this discussion took place on the assumption that there have been years of commitment to

certain kinds of development around the world which have miscarried
in the sense that even though there might be more food, there was
more poverty and not enough ability on the part of the majority of
people to buy the additional food that was produced. We started off
raising the question of the appropriateness of research in the universities with respect to the structures and systems that often are the
problem when it comes to getting food to the people that need food.
Many of the things said then were intended as matters of emphasis.
We want more of certain things and less of certain things. This is certainly not to say that the LGUs hadn't been doing a host of things that
were quite good and beneficial, but there is much more that can be
done so those benefits finally accrue to the hundreds of millions of
people in the world that are most in need.

I have a bias, too, that relates to my commitment to social justice.
If LGUs are to address the problems of eliminating hunger and
malnutrition in developing countries, they must give greatly increased
attention to the economic and political structures that have so often
kept the poor majorities in those countries from reaping the benefits
of agricultural research and development aid programs. The structures themselves, as well as the means of altering them, become proper
objects of social-scientific and moral inquiry.

UNITED STATES FOREIGN ASSISTANCE
summarized by Dieter T. Hessel

Land-grant universities have been involved in international
work for decades. Most of their funding has come through grants
from AID. In 1975, university personnel involved in international
work, in coalition with church groups concerned about world hunger,
successfully advocated passage of Title XII—Famine Prevention and
Freedom from Hunger, which became part of the amended Foreign
Assistance Act. In Title XII,

Congress declares that, in order to prevent famine and establish freedom
from hunger, various components must be brought together in order to increase world food production, including—

(1) strengthening the capabilities of universities to assist in increasing
agricultural production in developing countries;

(2) institution-building programs for development of national and
regional agricultural research and extension capacities in developing countries
which need assistance;

(3) international agricultural research centers;

(4) contract research; and

(5) research program grants.

The United States should—

(1) effectively involve the United States land grant and other eligible universities more extensively in each component;

(2) provide mechanisms for the universities to particiapte and advise in the planning, development, implementation, and administration of each component; and

(3) assist such universities in cooperative joint efforts with—

(A) agricultural institutions in developing nations, and

(B) regional and international agricultural research centers, directed to strengthening their joint and respective capabilities and to engage them more effectively in research, teaching, and extension activities for solving problems in food production, distribution, storage, marketing, and consumption in agriculturally underdeveloped nations.

Title XII specifically gives this mandate to the LGUs of the United States which "have demonstrable capacity in teaching, research, and extension activities in the agricultural sciences, and can contribute effectively to the [title's] objectives."

Title XII made money available (close to $200 million was authorized annually). The money was to be administered by a Board for International Agricultural Development, with two committees: (a) on research, and (b) on country programs. The board and its committees consist of representatives from land-grant and other universities. The board was appointed by and answerable to the president. There have been problems of transferring responsibility from AID to this structure, and a lack of clarity about the relationship between agricultural development and a more comprehensive development strategy.

More recently Congress has revised the act, incorporating proposals of the late Senator Hubert Humphrey. Humphrey proposed a more direct focus on the overall task of development assistance, with special attention to both economic and agricultural needs of the developing countries.

Title XII encourages LGUs to assist a "target" population of rural poor in the developing countries by creating and strengthening local institutions that focus on the special interrelated needs of small-farm agriculture. But LGUs have relatively little experience in building institutions that foster integrated rural agricultural development among the poor. Land-grant university research and extension in the United States has focused primarily on the economically competitive, "high tech," large-farm system.

Moreover, LGU faculty have only begun to venture into multidisciplinary approaches to social problem solving. If Title XII were to reinforce a mentality of "showing them how we do things at home," and if it were to accelerate the introduction and establishment of prevailing United States agricultural concepts in poor countries, it could have harmful effects on social justice and ecological conditions in developing countries. Responsible agricultural development must combine critical social insight with appropriate technical know-how in a way that serves the rural poor first of all.

Summary of priorities

1. Application of existing research rather than carrying out new research.

2. Spending of United States agricultural research dollars in developing countries.

3. Strengthening of research and extension institutions in the developing countries.

4. Training of agricultural research and extension personnel in developing countries.

5. Research on food crops.

6. Addressing the needs and constraints of poorer farmers.

7. Appropriate research and technology.

8. Targeting of United States agricultural research investments on specific problems in specific developing countries.

9. Channeling of funds through international institutions.

10. More effective integration of agricultural research within United States assistance policies toward developing nations.

11. Substantially increased funding for agricultural research.[1]

Problems of hunger and malnutrition cannot be solved by increasing production alone. These problems must be addressed through self-determined, self-sustaining processes of equitable development. A relevant development philosophy will emphasize that local social, political, economic, and cultural factors form a basic context that can foster or hinder authentic development. United States assistance should be tailored to the realities and needs of this basic context.

The United States land-grant system of research, teaching, and extension is uniquely suited, if properly engaged, to offer appropriate development assistance in a cooperative and interdisciplinary framework.   ●

CURRICULUM REFORM
a report by Lawrence Doerr

We spoke in tongues and on me fell the mantle of interpretation. We focused on Jerry Stockdale's statement that one's technology needs to be interwoven within the whole fabric of life. We understood that to mean that our vision and understanding will need to be focused on how we live and communicate responsively within a worldwide context. We need sensitivity to that wholeness of the fabric of life, as citizens of a global village. We need to build understanding, awareness, and to foster conscious choices about the values, the meanings, the perceptions, and the political and social biases by which we live with one another in this global village. We must learn something more than appreciation, something more than tolerance of the differing perceptions of reality and the differing technologies which exist side by side and contribute in the broadest sense to our basic interdependence.   ●

INFORMAL DISCUSSION

Hadwiger: It's a committee poem. I can't believe it. What was that last statement one more time?

Doerr: I don't think I can read it because it's not down in front of me here in that many words. I'm translating the tongues. Was there something out of it that was not clear?

Hadwiger: Something about "more than tolerance."

Doerr: We experimented with the term "tolerance," and experimented with the word "appreciation." And neither one of those clearly expressed the differing perceptions of reality, existing side by side; and also parallel to that, the notion of differing technologies—in the widest sense of the word—which contribute to the interdependent settings in which we live. We were suggesting that in the general area of curriculum reform (which we defined in extremely broad terms and with the caveat not to confuse schooling with education) this whole realm of the development of understanding, perception, and sensitivity was everyone's need—not just students in agriculture or in international work, but all students, all faculty, all people in our body politic. We touched on the whole question of the core curriculum that is being discussed in a lot of places in our society with its emphasis on some of the precise issues that we were raising. We talked about the role of advisers, mentors, and faculty-student relations as critical. So is the style and the vision by which a person teaches. For example, it may be more important for a person who teaches a course in soil science to do so within a perspective of alternatives, world realities, and politics, than it is for a person to offer a separate course that would "teach values." So one cannot merely talk about adding courses or putting in a new curriculum.

These are some of the specific suggestions that emerged from our discussion.

(1) Could it be that the primary role of the foreign students and their presence in our universities is to make international students out of our domestic students? Still, the economic and political selectivity by which foreign students come to us means that they are not the only influences we can and need to evaluate. So one gets into the rationales for such things as the junior year abroad programs, and the kinds of learning processes that Bill Rogers stresses, that gets us into acquaintance and relationship with people who will not come here as foreign graduate students in our technical schools. But nevertheless, we want to underline that one of the fundamental values of having foreign students here is the way they can help make our own students international in outlook.

(2) We want to identify, support, and reward the maverick—the creative teacher. Mavericks need nurturing communities and these are the relationships which we in the ministry can foster.

(3) We addressed ourselves to the role of continuing education and the extension network which reaches out and touches the lives of people in our community from the time they're children, on up through all of life. Where does this kind of concern for developing the broad vision, understanding, sensitivity get reinforced in the continuing education and extension programs? And how do the networks of churches and the networks of continuing education and extension programs, coupled with educational television, work together to get this kind of socially responsive education or this kind of enlightened "curriculum" developed? A good deal of this already happens, but the churches do not often see this as a way to express some of their concerns and commitments. For instance, shared with us last night was the material of the University of Mid-America's program on world food problems. Now that was done on educational TV in the state of Nebraska, and I am not aware of any church that responded by saying, "Here's an opportunity for us to educate and to broaden the vision of our people, and to use this TV program as an educational tool within the local congregation or within the local community as a strategy of the local church." One of the services that the CM might

be challenged to perform is that of coordinator between these networks that exist and make each aware of the other's strengths.

Knowles: From my own bias, I still think that professional competence is extremely important. I don't mean I'm going to specify
what courses you should have, but anybody going into a developing
nation to help must have professional competence. It helps the people
you're serving; it helps the person who's doing the job.

Doerr: Yes, professional competence is essential, but if you have
only professional competence, you'd better stay home.

C. Baker: We concluded that professional competence is a
necessary condition, but it isn't enough.

Doerr: I want to observe that change initiated by the process of
adding courses (whether required or not), or of having mavericks
within the situation, or of looking for creative teachers will tend to be
marginal in its effects it is not if reinforced by the style of the institution or department or faculty in the process of living with each other.
Take the question of the maverick. A maverick can either be a person
who for all of his/her abrasiveness is still obviously treasured and
recognized for making a positive contribution, or the maverick can be
someone forced to live on the edge. The message to students is that the
system is not really interested in what the maverick has to say, and we
must go to the edge to listen to him. So unless your system supports
these people, however abrasive they are, their value is limited.

STRATEGIC IMPLICATIONS FOR CAMPUS MINISTRY
a report by Donald Nead

The fourth group dealt with the strategic implications for
the CM, and our first recommendation built on an item that came out
of the group on curriculum reform.

(1) There is a need for an increased awareness of the possibilities
of collaboration between the church's CM and the LGU through the
cooperative extension services. This collaboration should be fostered
by an expansion of the services in home economics. Also, there is a
possible role for extension services in sensitizing constituencies on
world food issues and on the problem of world hunger. Extension services might be good allies in CROP projects, as well as in promoting
awareness of nutritional needs. Moreover, there is a need for increased dialogue between farm and nonfarm people in the life of the
church, as well as in the larger community. Perhaps church-extension
services could cooperate on programs of education, as well as
dialogue, centering on such issues as farm marketing, USDA policies,
new farming technologies, and the problem of commodities.

(2) There is a consciousness-raising task that needs to be done to help feel the impact of "imperialism," whether urban-rural or developed-underdeveloped. The LGU and CM should explore ways in which that can be done; namely, How do you sensitize people to certain policies and practices that produce feelings of "powerlessness" in our corporate life?

(3) Land-grant university education for international students is still a form of "colonialism" or "western imperialism." Though more sophisticated than the raw "ugly American" in its impact, LGU education nevertheless still implies an importing of western values and American "know how." Perhaps LGU and CM can explore ways of lifting that bias up to some exposure, so that there is at least an awareness of other possibilities.

(4) In local churches adjacent to the campus of LGUs, the role of preaching might be stressed as a way of lifting up the parallels and contrasts between the LGU purposes and the mission of the church. It might be well for the preachers to remind people of the purpose of the LGU in a very direct way.

(5) Another concern centered around the need to alert, inform, and sensitize faculty and staff of LGUs who are going overseas. Campus ministers can help to provide them with a perspective, or another set of glasses, through which to observe. This would be particularly true for those who claim a church affiliation, perhaps even going to the point of securing church contacts in the overseas situation so that additional learning may occur.

Caution! In some international situations, extreme caution should be used in seeking out nationals, particularly in countries where military dictatorships prevail, and where the Christian community is involved in some way with the forces for liberation. There is a danger of violating personal security, if blundering Yankees move into sensitive areas with little or no awareness of what is happening.

(6) The documents and papers from this consultation need to be shared with the broader network of LGUs and CMs so that they might be alerted to the emerging emphases and concerns. They should be invited to make some response by naming a campus minister and at least one faculty member to an ongoing network of citizens concerned over world hunger.

(7) Campus ministries and LGUs should be receptive to the insights of outside groups and to faculty within the system who seek a more appropriate agriculture. The reports of such groups and persons should inform further dialogue on the issues raised in this consultation. Land-grant university students may also be able to develop internships with domestic "responsible agriculture" groups.

(8) We recommend that we develop a Student World Hunger Intern Program that would be modeled on the Mission Intern Program of the Board of Global Ministries of the United Methodist Church. Interns are recruited to spend a year in a learning situation in a developing nation and then return to a receiving community in the United States for a two-year period of teaching and sharing.

(9) There is a necessity to center continuing scrutiny of our consultation and its concerns in a small network of persons who would help to coordinate, shape, and enable the further development of this ministry in UMHE.

(10) We recommend a series of regional meetings as a follow-up to this consultation, initiated by persons attending this meeting. We should expand the focus, be more ecumenical, but keep the target on LGUs. We should involve Third World persons as participants, as well as bringing in students. Seven regional conferences, hosted at LGUs, are planned for 1979 and following. Details are available from UMHE c/o Myrvin A. Delap, 1100 Witherspoon Building, Philadelphia, Pennsylvania 19107.   ●

INFORMAL DISCUSSION

Knowles: Of particular interest to me is the student internship. What is the church doing to encourage students in universities to be agricultural missionaries or to contribute to the improvement of developing nations? There's a good deal of interest on the part of students; the Peace Corps' success is evidence of this. I've had a few students come to me, wondering how they could get involved. One mentioned that he didn't see any opportunity in his own church and had decided to go abroad on the program of another church. These students are idealistic, they've got lots of energy, and I think they could be effective. Is the Presbyterian church doing very much in this regard? And when you do encourage them, do you have programs in which they can participate? From your remarks the answer is no.

Nead: The answer is yes, to a degree. It's not as extensive perhaps as it could be, but we have Volunteers in Mission, with an annual publication, as well as a selected set of interim publications to keep us informed about what is available through that kind of structure. Then through the UMHE, many of us have access into the volunteer systems of other denominations.

Knowles: Does your hunger program stress that you are going to encourage student participation?

J. Conner: That's the point of the recommendation.

Hessel: There was an alternative notion of a regional gathering, suggested by Norm Pott, which involves a mix of several, reasonably close campuses. Maybe that has more strategic priority. What exactly was your proposal on the regional conferences?

Nead: It would be to bring together a group similar to this consultation in the various regions. It was to be expanded in several directions; to bring in faculty and staff persons of the LGUs, campus ministers from UMHE structure, as well as Third World people and students.

Hessel: That should be ecumenically funded, not just Presbyterian.

Miner: We didn't specify the source of money.

Hessel: What is the responsibility of land-grant schools in terms of financial help?

Miner: Well, they release their people.

Hessel: That's all?

Nead: We didn't deal with that one.

C. Baker: I thought I heard you say something different about the students who might go into Third World countries. I thought you said something about their going in the role of learners, rather than as missionaries.

Nead: Right. I think there are two styles. The one we're recommending in this intern program is that they would go as learners and then come back and instruct us.

Knowles: What year in schooling are you talking about—the graduate? The sophomore? What stage in a student's career?

Nead: If it's modeled on the Methodist program, most of them are already graduates with some proficiency in the language of the country to which they're going. They cover the gamut of religious backgrounds. Most of them have had undergraduate work.

C. Baker: I want to bring up the domestic phase in which you suggest that clergy and consumers enter into dialogue with farmers for mutual instruction. I think also we should regard this as a learner model, and we should listen to their ideas.

Nead: The dialogue model is what we were talking about; it's a two-way dialogue.

B. Baker: One other concern we talked about. Students and faculty sent overseas by the LGU should be put in touch or know where they can get in touch with church people in the area—at university expense rather than church expense—and see what's going on after they actually get there.

Stockdale: This project of sending volunteers—I think there would be an advantage in having them go before they graduate, so that they could come back and share some of their experiences with their fellow students.

Nead: Yes, there are several different models that could be developed.

J. Conner: Each participant in the consultation has linkages in the church and in the university. We know that the reality of hunger has implications for us vocationally, professionally, and in terms of our own faith. How do we put some legs on our concern? Each of us can do something on our own campuses; whether we can do it in conjunction with another campus is another thing. We should be much more alert to the existing vocational, professional, and disciplinary resources in our own midst to enhance the work of those committees as they engage in education, information, sensitization, and action in a variety of ways.

Knowles: Speaking for myself and for the rest of us, I want to thank you, John, the staff, George Beran, and others locally for making this meeting such a success.

J. Conner: I want to thank you all for your participation. We have taken a step along the way, a partial realization of a dream that I have had for some time—to encourage the kind of dialogue which has gone on here. It enables us to respond more imaginatively to World Hunger. I am impressed by the items explored and the strengthening of our common concern, both in academia and in the church, to act for change.

NOTES

PREFACE

1. Cf. Dieter T. Hessel, "Solidarity Ethics: A Public Focus for the Church," *Review of Religious Research* 20 (1979): 3.

CHAPTER 1. Introduction

1. U.S., Congress, House, Committee on Agriculture, Subcommittee on Department Operations, *Malthus and America,* 93d Cong., 2d sess., October 1974, pp. 8, 15–16.

CHAPTER 2. Justice, the Church, and the Land-Grant University

1. C. Dean Freudenberger and Joseph C. Hough, Jr., "Lifeboats and Hungry People," in *Beyond Survival: Bread and Justice in Christian Perspective,* ed. Dieter T. Hessel (New York: Friendship Press, 1977), p. 32.
2. Ibid., p. 35.
3. Reinhold Niebuhr, *Justice and Mercy,* ed. Ursula M. Niebuhr (New York: Harper & Row, 1974), p. 36.
4. Dorothee Soelle, *Political Theology,* trans. John Shelley (Philadelphia: Fortress Press, 1974), p. 89.
5. Cited by Thomas J. Poleman, "World Food: A Perspective," *Science* 188 (1975): 515.
6. Joseph Collins and Frances Moore Lappé, "Still Hungry After All These Years," *Mother Jones* (August 1977): 31.
7. Ibid., p. 30; see the authors' *Food First: Beyond the Myth of Scarcity* (Boston: Houghton Mifflin, 1977).
8. Dorothee Soelle, "Remembering Christ: Faith, Theology and Liberation," *Christianity and Crisis* 36, no. 10 (June 7, 1976): 139. Emphasis added.
9. Denis Goulet, "World Hunger: Putting Development Ethics to the Test," *Christianity and Crisis* 35 (1975): 128.
10. "Human Hunger and the World Food Crisis," A Policy Statement of the National Council of Chruches of Christ in the United States of America, Adopted by the Governing Board October 11, 1975. The complete text may be found in Dieter T. Hessel, ed., *The Hunger Education/Action Manual* (New York: National Council of Churches, 1977).

CHAPTER 3. Appropriate Agricultural Technologies and Land-Grant Universities

1. T. M. Arndt, D. G. Dalrymple, and V. W. Ruttan, eds., *Resource Allication and Productivity in Natinal and International Agricultural Research* (Minneapolis: University of Minnesota Press, 1977).
2. Food and Agriculture Organization. *Resolutions Adopted by the World Food Conference and Report of the World Food Conference to the General Assembly, Rome.* 1974.
3. Frank Schaller, ed., *Proceedings of the World Food Conference.* World Food Institute, June 27–July 1, 1976. 1977. Ames: The Iowa State University Press.
4. U.S., Congress, House, Committee on Foreign Affairs, Subcommittee on International Organizations and Movements and on Foreign Economic Policy, *U.S. Policy and World Food Needs: Hearings before,* Cong., sess., September 10–12, 1974.
5. U.S. Congress, House, Committee on Science and Technology, Subcommittee on Science, Research and Technology and Subcommittee on Domestic and International Scientific Planning and Analysis, *Agricultural Research and Development: Hearings before,* Cong. sess., June 25–26; September 23–25, 30, 1975.
6. U.S., Congress, House, Committee on Science and Technology, Subcommittee on Science, Research and Technology and the Subcommittee on Domestic and International Scientific Planning and Analysis, *Special Oversight Review of Agricultural Research and Development: Special Oversight Report No. 2,* Cong., sess., 1976.
7. Report of the Committee on Research Advisory to the U.S. Department of Agriculture, National Research Council. 1974. Washington, D.C.: National Academy of Sciences.
8. S. H. Wittwer, *Research Recommendations for Increasing Food, Feed and Fiber Production in the U.S.A.,* (Washington, D.C.: National Science Foundation, 1974).
9. *Crop Productivity—Research Imperatives: Proceedings of an International Conference.* 1976. Michigan State University Agricultural Experiment Station, Charles F. Kettering Foundation.
10. Working Conference, Kansas City, Missouri, July 9–11, 1975. U.S., Department of Agriculture, Research to Meet U.S. and World Food Needs. I—The World Food Situation; II—Public Policy and Research Capabilities; III—Research Needs.
11. Report of the Board on Agriculture and Renewable Resources, National Research Council. *World Food and Nutrition Study: Enhancement of Food Production in the United States.* 1975. Washington, D.C.: National Science Foundation.
12. Report of the Steering Committee, National Research Council. *World Food and Nutrition Study: The Potential Contributions of Research.* 1977. Washington, D.C.: National Science Foundation.

13. Energy Research and Development Administration 1976. Report of the Proceedings of the Energy Research and Development Administration Workshop on Energy Conservation in Agricultural Production, July 15-16, 1976. Washington, D.C.

14. U.S., Congress, Office of Technology Assessment, *Assessment of Alternatives for Supporting High Priority Basic Research to Enhance Food Production.* 1977. Washington, D.C.

15. T. C. Edens, *Agricultural Management in a New Era: The Role of Insect Survey and Detection.* December 1977. The Entomological Society of America.

16. Consultative Group on International Agricultural Research. *Report of the Review Committee.* 1977. Washington, D.C.

17. E. F. Schumacher, *Small Is Beautiful: Economics as if People Mattered* (New York: Harper & Row, 1973).

18. Board on Science and Technology for International Development, Commission on International Relations, National Research Council. *Appropriate Technologies for Developing Countries.* Prepared by Richard Eckaus for the Panel on Appropriate Technologies for Developing Countries. 1977. Washington, D.C.: National Academy of Sciences.

19. S. H. Wittwer, "Increased Crop Yields and Livestock Productivity," in *World Food Prospects and Agricultural Potential* (New York: Praeger, 1977), pp. 66-135.

20. T. W. Schultz, *On Economics, Agriculture, and the Political Economy.* Elmhirst Lecture, International Conference of Agricultural Economics, July 26-August 6, 1976. Nairobi, Kenya.

21. The author expresses appreciation to Denton Morrison, professor of Sociology, Michigan State University, for his suggestions and some of the wording in this paragraph.

CHAPTER 6. Agriculture and Food Policy: Curricular Considerations

1. John H. Bodley, *Victims of Progress* (Menlo Park, Calif.: Cummings Publishing Co. 1975).

2. Angus Campbell, P. E. Converse, and W. L. Rogers, *The Quality of American Life: Perceptions, Evaluations and Satisfactions* (New York: Russell Sage Foundation, 1976)

3. The term "hidden curriculum" is adapted from use by David Light and S. I. Keller in *Sociology* (New York: Alfred A. Knopf, 1975), pp. 456. Light and Keller may have gotten the term from Phillip Jackson's book, *Life in Classrooms* (New York: Holt, Rinehart and Winston, 1968), but I did not attempt to trace previous use of the term.

4. David L. Armstrong, "Faculty Development" in David L. Armstrong, ed., *Impacts of Enrollments and Student Body Composition on Academic Program, Design and Delivery: A RICOP Report* (East Lansing, Mich.: Michigan State University, 1977), pp. 217-226.

CHAPTER 10.   Next Steps for Church and University

1. A rationale for these recommendations is available from the Inter-religious Task Force on U.S. Food Policy, 110 Maryland Ave., N.E., Washington, D.C. 20002.

INDEX